Cultivating Reality

Cultivating Reality

How the Soil Might Save Us

Ragan Sutterfield

CASCADE *Books* · Eugene, Oregon

CULTIVATING REALITY
How the Soil Might Save Us

Cascade Books
An Imprint of Wipf and Stock Publishers
199 W. 8th Ave., Suite 3
Eugene, OR 97401

www.wipfandstock.com

ISBN 13: 978-1-59752-656-2

Cataloging-in-Publication data:

Ragan Sutterfield.

Cultivating reality : how the soil might save us / Ragan Sutterfield.

viii + 122 p.; 23 cm—Includes bibliographical references.

ISBN 13: 978-1-59752-656-2

1. Agriculture—United States. 2. Agriculture—Social aspects. 3. Agriculture—Religious aspects—Christianity. I. Title.

HD1761 .S89 2013

Manufactured in the USA.

To my parents, for showing me the real

Table of Contents

1

The Soteriology of Soil

"There are two spiritual dangers in not owning a farm. One is the danger of supposing that breakfast comes from the grocery and the other that heat comes from the furnace."
—Aldo Leopold

I look forward to February because it is in that month, with the days still short and cold, that the hope of spring begins. We start plants in seed trays, sprouting and nurturing them in window sills and greenhouses, getting ready for the late days of March and early April when the Arkansas garden season begins with force. It is in February that I also begin to work the soil, to add compost and manure, and nurture the ground that is necessary for any good gardening. Beneath the soil, billions of microbes take the nutrients I add and build whole networks and systems of life. It is these microbes that will deliver much needed nitrogen to the roots of the plants; it is this living soil that is the beginning of any good growth. We call this soil humus and it is connected to the very nature of ourselves as humans, reflecting the Hebrew idea that *adam* (humankind) was formed from the *adamah* (humus). We are essentially humus-beings—people who gain our life from and are completely dependent upon dirt. This is a truth we can deny only at our peril.

But what does this mean for Christians and what does it mean for the church? How are we to address this reality in our anthropology that is always modeled on the example and person of Christ? Here I want to argue why a thing called agrarianism—a habit of mind formed through the understanding that our lives are dependent upon the soil—is important for the church, particularly in this age and time. I want to show that the church needs agrarianism to help it recall and articulate its implicit anthropology and ecology.

This is not a book where we will explore the specific thinking of particular agrarians, since there are already many good books that have done so, but rather this is an exploration of some common agrarian themes with an eye to how those themes might speak to Christian communities and their members. We begin with the basics: reality.

Not long ago, I had a conversation, by old fashioned handwritten letter, with my friend Fred Bahnson. Fred is a farmer, writer, and sometime preacher. Fred believes that farming is an essential human practice and vocation, perhaps our most fundamental work. What concerned Fred in this particular letter was how to express to Christians the importance of the agrarian habit of mind—the critical nature of questions of farming, food, and table to our Christian life. I thought a good deal about Fred's concern and it occurred to me that what agrarianism is really about is living in the truth—it is realism at its best. The call to Christians to learn from agrarians is then a call to Christians to form a habit of mind that will deepen our sense of reality. And this is essentially what salvation is—a deliverance from false realities into full reality as embodied in Christ. Agrarianism can help Christians embrace this salvation. As Fred wrote, "I think the agrarian life, grounded as it is in reality, is capable of bringing people out of Babylon and training them to live in the New Jerusalem."

This salvific potential of agrarianism may seem a bold claim. The church after all has long been in the salvation business—how can agrarianism with its attention to dirt and gardens and livestock help save the church? As Fred indicated, it is in its very grounding, its attention to these basic, physical realities of life that agrarianism can help call us "out of Babylon" and train us "to live in the New Jerusalem."

The church has lived in a constant struggle throughout its history to escape from the grounded realities of dirt. The "spiritual life" has become its domain and whether explicitly stated or not, salvation has come to mean the deliverance of souls and not bodies, persons not planets. We have come to ignore the God who promises the deliverance of a world and hope for the nations, the God who saves a people whose work is to deliver the creation that is waiting in eager longing for these people to embrace their call.

When we forget that God wants to save creation, and we deny our vocation to join God in this work, we are brought into false realities—powerful idolatries that lead us away from seeing the truth of ourselves, God, and the creation of which we are members. We need concrete practices that will cultivate our ability to live in reality, practices that will enable us to stand on reality's firm ground rather than eventually crash into its hard edge. Agrarianism is simply a name for habits of mind and body that call us to the most significant intersection of our life and the life of the whole of creation—the table at which we eat.

The reality of the table has been a changing one, one marked by illusions and idolatries that the church has far too often done little to unveil, bowing our heads at the golden arches rather than the golden calf. Rather than the table being a place where we eat the abundance God has provided us through the careful management and cultivation of creation, our tables are now filled with foods that are wreaking havoc on our bodies and the creation. These foods are abundant, but their abundance is dependent on a mining of nutrients from the soil, the abuse of animals, and the exploitation of people. Agrarians call this form of false abundance "industrialism," a form of economy that is the antonym of an economy based on craft and cultivation.

An Economy of Icons or an Economy of Idols?

In describing the industrial economy as opposed to the agrarian one, it might be helpful to borrow the images of idol and icon from the philosopher Jean-Luc Marion. As Bruce Benson describes Marion's concept of idol and icon, "the idol is something that merely reflects our gaze, [while] the icon points our sight to something beyond it and thus to something beyond ourselves that we cannot master."[1] The industrial economy is an economy of the idol. It reflects the gaze of our false understandings, twisted through disordered desires and addictions. Value in this economy is dictated through supply and demand, both easily manipulated through property systems and advertising. This is the economy of consumerism, driven by demand whatever those demands are. The agrarian economy on the other hand is an economy of the icon. It is an economy where value is received rather than made; its absolute measure always tenuous. An economy of the icon sees the world as a place of abundance rather than scarcity and it does not propose to name every good within it.

Perhaps the best agrarian statement on the economies of the idol and the icon is Wendell Berry's essay, "Two Economies." Berry describes a conversation he had with fellow agrarian Wes Jackson about a better way to determine value than that offered by the money economy. Berry proposed that an economy based on a measure of energy would be preferable, but Jackson disagreed, saying that such a measure is still not broad enough. "Then what kind of economy *would* be comprehensive enough?" Berry asked. Jackson "hesitated a moment, and then grinning, said, 'The Kingdom of God.'"[2]

Berry goes on to agree with Jackson, because the "kingdom of God" does properly name an economy whose scale of value is comprehensive enough to fit with reality. "The thing that troubles us about the industrial economy," writes Berry, "is exactly that it is not comprehensive enough, that moreover, it tends to destroy what it does not comprehend, and that it is *dependent* upon much that it does not comprehend." These statements are exactly the statements

1. Benson, "Jean-Luc Marion," 22.
2. Berry, *Home Economics*, 54.

we could make of an idol—the problem of an idol, whether made of concrete or concepts, is that it is not comprehensive enough, that it limits the divine to our outlines and understanding, and yet an idol is also dependent upon what we cannot understand—it is able to maintain its pretensions toward divinity because of the borrowed light that it mirrors and mimics.

The answer to the industrial economy, writes Berry, is "an economy that does not leave anything out, and we can say without presuming too much that the first principle of the Kingdom of God is that it includes everything; in it, the fall of every sparrow is a significant event."[3] Like an icon, whose image cannot contain what is represented, the agrarian economy within the Kingdom of God must operate within an economy, which including everything, "can never know either all the creatures . . . or the whole pattern or order."[4] Our position must be one of care and caution, just as a good Christian must be guided by a "fear of the Lord." This fear, to borrow a metaphor from Dallas Willard, is not because God is mean, but because God is dangerous.[5] God in this sense is like electricity—electricity is not malicious, but it is dangerous—woe to the one who takes it lightly. It is the same with the economy of the Kingdom of God. As Berry writes, "Though we cannot produce a complete or even adequate description of this order, severe penalties are in store for us if we presume upon it or violate it."[6]

To begin sorting out the economy of the idol and the icon, how the industrial economy and the agrarian economy play out, let us return to the table. Perhaps the best way to express how this might begin to happen is to say that agrarianism requires us to take account of and responsibility for our ignorance while industrialism claims that we have all the knowledge we need. There is no better way to explore this than in how both ways of seeing look at food.

3. Ibid., 55.
4. Ibid.
5. Willard, *Renovation*, 51.
6. Berry, *Home Economics*, 54–55.

At the Table with Our Ignorance

For agrarians we are responsible for our food whether we grow it or cook it ourselves or whether we let someone else do those things for us. An agrarian economy is centered on helping us become better at fulfilling those responsibilities rather than thwarting them. The ideal of the agrarian economy is a farmers market where farmers and customers are in close communication, the customers even working some with the farmers to get a better sense of how their food is grown. Questions are encouraged and openness and transparency are ideal. "How are the animals slaughtered?" is answered with "come see." "How are the crops grown" is answered with "come help."

In the industrial economy, however, food is divorced from its history. Apples may have labels of which countries they came from, but beyond the brief imagining of a plane ride there's no story that the customer can become a part of—it is a life in fragments. A supermarket, even at its edges where the food is most whole, is an end point of a great deal of processing and polishing. Vegetables are shrink-wrapped, apples waxed, carrots trimmed and cut so that whatever productive part we might play in the eating of our food is taken away. The goal is a product to be consumed.

On the other side of industrialism is a secretive system of agriculture that relies on the large scale production of starches and proteins that are endlessly reformed into the many food products that fill the shelves of grocery store aisles. From corn to pigs, the industrial system talks in terms of abstraction—Tyson is no longer a chicken and beef company, it is a protein company. Cargill doesn't raise pigs, it provides "protein solutions." Of course animals—literally beings with spirits—do not fit within such a model easily. The only way that they do "fit" is through an incredible level of abuse and violence that leads to chronic outbreaks of disease that must be fought with routine antibiotics, which in turn create resistant bacteria that seriously threaten human health.

A Life Lived Through Proxy

Most of us would be appalled at the violence that is inherent in the industrial system, but this violence is very difficult to see, even for those who participate in it, because in the industrial system each part is divorced from another so that wholes are made invisible. Against this, agrarianism would remind us that we are responsible for this violence to the degree that we enjoy its products. The burger we eat quickly on a road trip is directly tied to eroding corn fields in Illinois, the pesticide ridden tomato fields of Mexico, genetically modified soybeans in Arkansas, water depleting wheat fields in Nebraska, and lagoons of manure laced with antibiotics in Colorado. Agrarianism holds us responsible for these realities because one of the central ideas of agrarianism is that we live through proxies and we are responsible for our proxies.

A proxy is the transfer of one's agency to someone or something to act on one's behalf. For agrarians, when we purchase food we are not simply buying a product that begins and ends with the product, rather we are exchanging money to pay someone to provide food for us through proxy. If I don't grow a cow myself, but I eat beef, I am raising a cow through proxy. If that cow is abused that too is a part of my proxy—I am responsible for what is done on my behalf. My ignorance of such abuse is simply a witness to the poor management of my proxies or my irresponsibility rather than my lack of any responsibility at all. Our proxies extend to all of the basics of our life—the water we drink, the computers we use, the clothes we wear.

To take the discussion of proxies out of the context of food, let us look at computers like the one on which I am now writing. Many years ago, Wendell Berry made quite a stir when he wrote an essay published in *Harpers Magazine* explaining why he won't buy a computer.[7] Among the many reasons outlined was Berry's realization that this technology would require the use of the very polluting industries he was writing against. He admitted the he was not without contribution to destructive systems and economies, but that when it came to the choice of adding another way in which he

7. Berry, *What Are People For?*, 170–77.

would contribute (by buying a computer) he would do well to keep to what had already been working (writing by hand and working with his wife to type up his manuscripts on a manual typewriter). The essay generated a record number of responses to *Harpers*, many people seeming personally offended that Berry would question the ethics of buying a machine that is without argument filled with toxins and relies, for the most part, on huge amounts of electricity that is largely generated by coal burning or other environmentally damaging forms of power generation from nuclear to hydroelectric. At its heart, what people were reacting to was Berry's suggestion, scandalous as it was, that they had a responsibility for the products they buy and the companies who act as proxies for them.

Difficult as they may be to accept, the reality of proxies shows us in part why an urban dweller in New York City should care as much as a farmer in Illinois about the quality of soil and its erosion. Agrarianism is not just for farmers or rural people because though agrarianism is rooted in the traditions of both, the concerns of farmers and rural people should be the concerns of all of us. At the end of the day we are all dependent upon the soil and systems that preserve and nurture the soil. For agrarians we are all, to some degree, farmers, whether in practice or through proxy. When we say with the agrarians that we are all farmers we make a statement upon which we can be judged. It also gives us an ideal into which we can live—wherever we are and as we understand this role, and begin to take responsibility for our proxies, we will move from being ignorant consumers to skilled practitioners and producers. Some, like Slow Food founder Carlo Patrini, have even called for a vision of ourselves as co-producers rather than consumers. To become co-producers we must become active participants in the management of our proxies and this requires that we gain some of the experience and skills of farmers.

The local foods movement that has grown tremendously over the last decade has created a path for many to move from the role of consumer to co-producer. As people seek to be more deeply aware of the history of their food and care more and more that their food is a part of a good and truthful story, they also almost inevitably seek to begin growing some of their own food, raise their own chickens, and make good compost with the waste that comes from their kitchens. One begins to see people finding their vocation—the original human call to farm that at its best is the service of creation's flourishing. We are not called to be simply consumers, nor are we called to be extractive producers; we are called from the beginning to be cultivators.

The Priesthood of All Farmers, Or the Farmerhood of all People

During the Protestant Reformation Martin Luther articulated an often misunderstood view called "the priesthood of all believers." In this view Luther was not seeking to do away with the special vocation of priests, but rather to say that all of us who are Christians have a role to play as mediators of God's love and presence in the world. To say that we are all farmers is something like the idea of the "priesthood of all believers"—it is not the diminishment of the vocation of those who spend every day, day in and day out raising food, but rather it is to say that in this intersection of creation and culture that finds itself centered at the table we all have a role to play and a responsibility for our place in that role.

In thinking about what this can mean, I think of my friend Claudio Oliver in Brazil. Claudio lives in a neighborhood we'd call suburban, but he is doing some radical and subversive things there. He and several friends have begun an urban farming movement that ranges from apartments in the neighborhood to backyards where they are growing thousands of pounds of food, and better yet, they are taking in other people's trash and turning it into rich compost so that they can create more food. The people involved in this work are taking their role as farmers seriously; they are taking responsibility for their proxies.

By opening ourselves to a role as cultivators of creation, which is what farming at its best really is, we also open ourselves to wild engagement with the given world of which we are a part. If this is a world of abundance, well beyond our own ability to control or contain or even comprehend, then we should approach it as such.

This has two basic sides. On the one hand we should seek to make our farming more wild and on the other hand we should see our role as a cultivation of that wild. These two sides are what separate agrarianism from a kind of ecological vision that is focused purely on the preservation of a wilderness. The focus is instead on life in working landscapes that work for everything from soil microbes to people.

Gary Nabhan, an ethnobiologist who works with Native people in the Sonoran desert, has written about the desert oasis Quitobaquito.[8] This oasis was a traditional source of irrigation for the Tohono O'odham people, but was made a part of the Organ Pipe National Monument. The national monument is a preserve aimed at protecting the desert ecosystems and so the oasis was no longer available to the Tohono O'odham for irrigation. Just across the U.S.-Mexico border from the National Monument, the Tohono O'odham still use a very similar oasis for irrigation. The amazing thing is that the biodiversity of the oasis at the Organ Pipe National Monument has significantly declined since the time it became a "preserve" while the oasis still used by the Tohono O'odham thrives with a wide variety of native plants and wildlife.

These two oases illustrate the central agrarian vision that nature is not better off without people, but that people have a key role to play within the landscape when they fulfill their proper role as cultivators. Unfortunately, we have not been servants of the land encouraging its flourishing and have instead been miners of value from the landscape. National Parks, conservancies, and preserves are the natural flipside of an economy based on extraction—an economy that sees cultivation as the role of specialists rather than a skill and responsibility that should be developed by all people.

Grace and Works

The kind of agriculture represented by the Tohono O'odham is both placed and small scale—it is agriculture that has been developed by people living on the land for centuries. Large scale agriculture of

8. Nabhan, *The Desert.*

the sort that began in the Fertile Crescent some ten thousand years ago is of an entirely different kind, a form of agri-mining rather than agri-culture, based on the presumption of manufactured abundance that recalls the ambitions of Babel. From the beginning, agriculture of this sort resulted in massive soil erosion and began the cycles of prosperity and famine that are still with us today.

There is evidence that some ancient people were forming and managing their food supply in ways other than this extractive agriculture. Like hunters today, Paleolithic people most likely managed their landscapes and even cultivated plants in order to attract game. They were more akin to wildlife managers than farmers, but it is also key to note that their role was not inactive on the landscape. There are some archeologists that even suggest that large parts of the Amazon Rainforest were "designed"—a wild garden that provided an abundance of food for the people there as chronicled in books like *The Lost City of Z* and *1491*.

This is perhaps a better image of our call as cultivators—wildlife managers rather than corn farmers on a combine. This vision brings with it a kind of humility. Our modern agricultural systems would like to imagine that with the right kind of inputs, the right sort of genetically modified seed, we can simply come to the soil and make something grow. But in the agrarian vision there is a dance of effort and grace to the work of farming, an acceptance of givens as much as a manufacturing of sustenance. We must be prepared to receive the grace of growth and flourishing when it comes, but that grace cannot be made. It is a gift that we must receive.

One might think that this sense of grace would lead to a fatalistic view of agriculture—a sense like that of some of the members of Paul's churches that grace ensured that they were not required to work toward goodness. Yet agrarianism, trained as it is in the real work of farming, is certainly attached to the need to work. But this work is always tempered by the understanding that it cannot be finished or complete in itself—that the work is tied up with a whole gathering of beings and that the work is not that of a prison camp where it is forced, but is rather like a barn raising where labor is focused on accomplishing one task because it is part of a greater whole. Work in the agrarian vision must be answered with idleness in an appropriate rhythm.

In the agrarian vision we work to fulfill our responsibility as people, but it is not the be all and end all of our being or the final source of our sustenance. As farmers know, the hardest work can still result in a crop failure or other catastrophe. It is a rejection of that reality that has driven industrial agriculture in an effort to ensure against unpredictable harvests—its model is not mercy but control of the variables. For those who grew up when such failures were real possibilities one can certainly understand the desire, but rather than accepting with humility the reality of mercy and grace, industrialism has struck a Faustian bargain for predictable harvests—poisoned aquifers, fossil fuel dependency, and rural unemployment. After all of this, industrial agriculture is extremely vulnerable to market fluctuations of fuel and fertilizers. Such agriculture simply couldn't survive without a huge subsidy system.

The New Monasteries of the New Dark Ages

At the close of Alasdair MacIntyre's *After Virtue* he comments that our world, like that of the Romans before us, is being sacked by the barbarians. The trouble for us, MacIntyre says, is that we are unaware that the barbarians are in charge. This describes the industrial economy—an economy where value as a category has been significantly perverted. When something like a mortgage default swap can be profitable (at least for a time) and growing good food from the earth is not profitable, something has gone seriously askew—the barbarians are in charge.

The answer, says MacIntyre, is not all that different from the way that Western Civilization was saved from the Dark Ages:

> What matters at this stage is the construction of local forms of community within which civility and the intellectual and moral life can be sustained through the new dark ages which are already upon us. And if the tradition of the virtues was able to survive the horrors of the last dark ages, we are not entirely without grounds for

hope. This time however the barbarians are not waiting beyond the frontiers; they have already been governing us for quite some time. And it is our lack of consciousness of this that constitutes part of our predicament. We are waiting not for a Godot, but for another—doubtless very different—St. Benedict. [9]

St. Benedict, of course, was the founder of Western monasticism and it was his "schools for Christlikeness" that many historians agree were refuges of civility and the preservers of culture as the structures of the Roman Empire fell apart. We need a new Benedict and new communities to preserve craft in the face of the very real catastrophe that awaits us.

Agrarianism provides a vision for what these small communities might look like. As Gene Logsdon writes, "Sustainable farms are to today's headlong rush toward global destruction what monasteries were to the Dark Ages—places to preserve human skills and crafts until some semblance of common sense and common purpose returns to the public mind." [10]

Like the New Monastic movement, the agrarian resurgence provides a vision for a new/old kind of community that helps remind us what it means to be human. In this, we might say that agrarianism is not only realism at its best, but also a kind of humanism. Its aim is to celebrate and remind us what being human means—not a life of gainful employment marketing products for a company whose manufacturing practices in some foreign place are destroying the world, but gifted beings created from the earth and granted, from the mouth of God, the breath of life. This agrarian vision of what we might call humanistic environmentalism was expressed well by Michael Braungart, a chemist, designer and co-author of the book *Cradle to Cradle.* "I can tell you, sustainability is boring," wrote Braungart, "It is just the minimum. Like when you were asked: 'How is your relationship with your girlfriend?' What do you say? Sustainable? I'd say: 'I am so sorry for you.' . . . Instead

9. MacIntyre, *After Virtue*, 263.

10. Logsdon, *Living*, xxi.

we should celebrate being human beings and our creativity, which is far more important than sustainability."[11]

Holistic vs. Industrial Environmentalism

This humanistic vision not only opens us up to a more Christian and joyful environmentalism, but it also helps to protect us from the increasing utilitarianism being expressed by some environmentalists. In such a utilitarian approach holism is scrapped for an industrial approach that isolates goals and targets very specific solutions. This industrial environmentalism is concerned with solving particular problems rather than a wholesale lifestyle change toward living at nature's pace. It is interested in conserving water, but not conserving farms. It is interested in stopping global warming, but willing to sacrifice an ecologically significant river for a hydroelectric dam.

This industrial environmentalism is convenient for the greening of corporations. A corporation can become "green" by picking any single problem, creating some solution to it, and going about destroying the ecosystem in every other aspect of its work. As an example, Monsanto has recently embarked on a "sustainability" campaign focused on creating Genetically Modified corn, soybeans and cotton that will yield twice as much as current seeds and will use 30 percent less water. This is a wonderful thing from the perspective of industrial environmentalism, meaning less land could be used for growing more crops and fewer water resources would be required for double the yield.

But there is a central problem here and it becomes apparent when we step out of the realm of the simple logic of utilitarianism. "If the earth is holy, then the things that grow out of the earth are also holy. They do not belong to man to do with them as he will."[12] These lines from L. H. Bailey's conservation classic, *The Holy Earth*, cuts through all of the instrumentalism of Monsanto's tired PR strategy that it is helping feed the world, improve the lives of the poor, and better the environment while at the same time acquiring

11. Braungart, "Population."
12. Bailey, *The Holy Earth*, 12.

a monopoly on seed and suing farmers whose plants do what plants do and cross-pollinate.

For Bailey the Earth is something beyond us, something that was here before us, something that we are a part of rather than possess. Monsanto uses biotechnology to create plants that cannot reproduce after the first generation and then patents the resulting genetic code, betraying the agrarian tradition of seed saving and the free availability of genetic material. Yes, we must solve human problems, but we must do it without stepping out of the basic rules of nature and we should proceed with great caution when determining what and where those rules lie. As Bailey writes, "A good part of agriculture is to learn how to adapt one's work to nature, to fit the crop-scheme to the climate and to the soil and the facilities. To live in right relation with his natural conditions is one of the first lessons that a wise farmer or any wise man learns."[13] To be in "right relation" to our natural conditions, that is the heart of true conservation, it is the heart of the deepest tradition of environmentalism.

Integrity

When we ignore that tradition and the idea of "right relation" we simply participate in the same mindset that has always driven the destruction of the world. It is the mindset that says "nature isn't good enough." We have to do more than cultivate its natural dispositions according to its natural limits as we do in the traditional breeding of plants and animals. We have to change its fundamental DNA because nature as given doesn't meet our needs—the limits of nature are too confining.

Agrarianism is then a call to integrity—to life and action lived without divide and without hypocrisy, where a right relationship to nature translates into a right relationship with work and a right livelihood. "If 'the earth is the Lord's' and we are His stewards," writes Berry, "then obviously some livelihoods are 'right' and some are not."[14] We cannot set out to make our living, if we are to be

13. Ibid., 7–8.
14. Berry, *Gift*, 275.

neighborly, by depriving and destroying our commonwealth—our common gift of good land. "Is there not, in Christian ethics," asks Berry, "an implied requirement of practical separation from a destructive or wasteful economy?"[15]

In calling us to integrity and a practical separation from a wasteful economy, agrarianism reminds us to live our lives on a proper scale—that the scope of our actionable care can only extend so far and to work in ways that reach beyond that scope will inevitably be destructive. The home and the parish—these are the levels at which our life should operate. Rather than seeking the big solutions we must first meet and answer the questions of our own lives, here.

A good illustration of this came in a brilliant strip from the online comic "Coffee with Jesus." Illustrated in a style reminiscent of sixties-era tracts, a woman is talking with Jesus complaining that world peace has not yet been accomplished. Jesus responds, "How about you learn to get along with your co-workers and ex-husband first? World peace is a few years off, sister."[16] The reply is the reply of agrarianism to the grand problem we face in the environment. If we don't live better lives, lives of greater integrity, then how can we call out the coal companies and oil companies for not answering our demands?

This principle of dealing with small things first is central to Jesus's teaching. In the Sermon on the Mount Jesus tells his disciples that if they are going to worship God, in other words get right with God, and remember on their way to the temple that they are not right with their neighbor, then they should first get right with their neighbor. Right relationships are central not only to ecology but the gospel, and we cannot expect to truly live into the kingdom of God if we don't live in right relationship to the creation which is the context of our collective neighborhood.

Agrarianism calls us to get right with our neighbors and our neighborhoods, and just as Jesus realized, it is through that action that the big changes come. World peace starts not with grand treaties, but with people learning to get right with the people they

15. Ibid.

16. Radio Free Babylon, "World Peace."

encounter every day. A healthy ecosystem starts when we quit driving, stop living in a throwaway economy, and start to turn waste into new soil and resources around our households. Write your congress persons, sure, for what little it's worth try to stop Babylon from being Babylon, but what matters more is that we care from a place of integrity and careful work—that we act from our homelands and parishes, places that extend to much smaller radius's than national borders built on the Enlightenment imperialist ambitions of manifest destinies.

The Soil Saves

When Fred Bahnson wrote in his letter that a care for the soil might save us, that agrarianism is "capable of bringing people out of Babylon and training them to live in the New Jerusalem" that might have seemed a big claim. But in a world filled with idols agrarianism offers us icons—visions and practices that open us to reality, which is the place that the God who is real lives.

We now live in Babylon—a culture of captivity—and most of us have become comfortable with life here. Food is available everywhere, clean water runs from our faucets, we can easily drive from one place to another, the economy for whatever its momentary woes still provides for the most part. To live here comfortably we only have to bow our heads and pay homage with our money to the manufactured abundance that makes up this kingdom. We have to preserve our ignorance and make sure that no one violates the sacred flow of oil or electricity that we simply cannot live without. What happens outside of Babylon is of no concern as long as Babylon is filled with abundance, wealth, and health.

But just as the Israelites were called out of their comfortable lives of accommodation, we too must leave this false world of manufactured abundance to live in the promise land. It is a land that might not seem so wonderful at first; our hands and feet and bodies are soft from lives lived in illusion. But once we've learned to live as human beings once more—to use our muscles, our minds, our hearts to engage with the humus from which we were formed, there will be no longing for Babylon, only for the full restoration of Jerusalem.

Salvation should surely be the business of the church, but our understanding of salvation has been formed by a desire to continue our lives in service to the idols of Empire. We have come to see salvation not as a radical call to live fully into reality, but rather a matter of the spiritual, a domain we can speak of passionately while letting its reality stay comfortably irrelevant.

Forget the salvation of the soul—let us preach God's salvation of human beings. To save human beings we must save the creation they are a part of because human life makes no sense without humus. The church needs agrarianism because the church needs dirt, the spirit needs a body or else it is just a ghost. It was the spirit of God given to humus that gave birth to the human. It is upon God and dirt that we are dependent.

2

Dependent, Limited Creatures

"The margins of our gardens can be tropes too, but
figures of irony rather than transcendence—
antidotes, in fact, to our hubris."
—MICHAEL POLLAN,
Second Nature: A Gardener's Education

Beside me my infant daughter Lily sits in her "bouncy chair." She's
asleep mostly, gurgling a bit, and I'm counting down the minutes
until she wakes. Lily is radically dependent—her neck too weak to
hold her head, her hands lacking the coordination to even keep a
pacifier in her mouth, her only food is her mother's milk. These
things will change of course—she will grow in strength, coordination, agility. She will be able, more and more, to do things without
the help of her mother and me. But she will not grow less dependent.

Already, Lily's dependence is growing daily, increasing in
breadth and complexity. With each kiss from Emily and me, with
each lick from our dog Maurice, with each exposure to a visitor or
time sitting outside, her body is becoming populated by bacteria
of an ever increasing variety. From lactobacilli to e coli her body
is becoming better able to digest a wider variety of food, preparing
her for taking in solids. Other bacteria are enabling her respira-
tion, others populating and protecting her skin. The variety and

complexity and role of all the organisms invading her body are not even understood.

When she begins to eat solids, simple foods like carrots and sweet potatoes and squash at first, she will become more directly intertwined in a whole network of life and death—the nutrient cycle of humus to humus, the cycle of water, the sun and air—exhalations exchanged. These networks are now mediated through my wife Emily who converts the plants and animals she eats into the milk that will nourish Lily, but in due time Lily will begin to be a part of this cycle as well.

Lily will also begin to move more freely and imitate, to talk. Her neural development is already dominated by the conversations she overhears and at a couple of months she is now beginning to have some intentionality to the gurgles she makes, her first attempts to communicate—literally to be with us in the full connection of mind and body.

As Lily's immune system develops we are glad that we at least have a couple of indoor pets. We hope to expose her to as much grass and dirt as possible over the summer. It is by interacting with a wide variety of people and animals that she will gain protection from many diseases of inflammation like allergies. Studies have shown that the lowest rates of allergies are found among people, such as the Amish, who have been raised on traditional farms with exposures to a variety of animals. Those in "sanitary conditions"— monocultural landscapes—are at the highest likelihood for a life of allergy shots.[1]

We need to live in multicultural spaces of dependence—varied life is what gives us health. Lily's growing dependence, the expanding network of creatures and people upon which she relies, is not a problem—it is growth itself. And what each of us experiences as we enter life only continues. Dependence is a gift without which we wouldn't be human.

1. Neighmond, "Allergies."

Being Made

Our dependence is rooted in our creatureliness. We have a beginning; we are made and not autonomous beings. In our createdness we also have limits—we cannot be whatever we want in life, however much our doting parents or teachers might suggest. We have limits of mind and body, of ability, of genetic potential. We also have limits of purpose and in that, limits of choice—it is upon these limits that our health is dependent.

This morning I had breakfast with a friend and we talked about the scope of the no's that had occurred in his life, the blessing of closed possibilities. "When I got married, it was like a thousand doors shutting. When I had my son, more doors slammed shut. But it was only with the closing of those possibilities that I could embrace the possibility of being a father or a husband." To embrace a purpose is to escape from choice and this is as it should be. Those who want to keep their options open, those who never want to settle down, are acting in denial of the basic realities of who they are as people—they are seeking personhood without humanity, a life of being without the borders that give definition. The idea of a self-made man is just as absurd. To make is to choose and none of us choose our existence—it is a given. We are the given-man and the given-woman. What we become is not a matter of making, but of how we accept the gift of being.

"The LORD God formed man from the dust of the ground, and breathed into his nostrils the breath of life; and the man became a living being" (Gen 2:7). Reading this passage now I can only think of the moment my daughter was born—a cough and gasp of air. Each of us is a participant in the same reality as the first formation of humankind, essentially born from the humus that is the source of the minerals, proteins, chemical building blocks that are captured by plants from the sun and soil and metabolized by animals and back to the soil again. From the beginning we are connected and created. And in this creation we find ourselves the subjects of an intention, a purpose.

"The LORD God took the man and put him in the garden of Eden to till it and keep it" (Gen 2:15). Our purpose is tied up with creation of which we are a part—our life lived properly is to be a life that serves (the Hebrew word for "till," *abad* can also mean serve) the garden and cultivates its flourishing. If we live within the limits of that cultivation we have the freedom to eat freely of its abundance, but if we violate our limits, we step outside of the possibilities of abundance.

The Human Form

To say that we have a purpose means that there is a kind of ideal shape of our lives to which we should conform. Our freedom is defined by our ability to enter into the pattern of this ideal—not to escape it. This reality is in some ways easiest to grasp on the level of our bodies. We are born with a significant level of possibility and limit. Our genes provide a sort of programming that guides the pattern of our growth, but increasingly it is understood that the expression of genes is heavily influenced by what we do. Twins who have identical genetic potential may end up living very different kinds of lives depending on the kinds of things they eat, the exercise they get, and other environmental influences. There is a kind of ideal in the genes, but the possibility of that expression is dependent on choices along the way.

We therefore have this dance again of effort and grace. A purpose is given to us, our lives are not absurd, but we can make them absurd by not living fully into our purpose. And all too often, our society abandons a meaningful existence within the bounds of our intended forms and limits, and accepts an absurd life of shallow freedom instead. This is especially true in our society's relationship to bodies, but what goes for our bodies can easily reflect the ecosystems of which they are a part.

"My body is a cage," goes a lyric of the band Arcade Fire, expressing a common sentiment. People speak of being trapped in their bodies, chained to them. As desire is uncoupled from the body, particularly in cyber-reality, this feeling can be accentuated even more. Of course the body eventually demands its own recognition, its limits come to bear, and so we have an increasing number of possible ways in which the limits of the body can be mitigated by surgery or drugs. Late pregnancy is just one example of this as drug companies seek ways to allow women to safely deliver children in their middle ages, potentially even into a woman's fifties. The natural limits of birthing age can be overcome, but at what expense?

Viagra too has served to extend the "pleasures of the body" whose demise Cephalus welcomes in the opening of Plato's *Republic* as an opportunity to embrace philosophical conversation. Our society is now so heavily medicated with drugs that enable us to escape natural limits, or deal with the consequences of escaping those limits, that our medicine itself has become a major source of pollution. Biologists are now seeing fish with extreme mutations, such as male fish with ovaries, as a result of the hormone based birth control, Prozac, Viagra, and other common drugs that make their way into our waterways through our sewage. Rather than our waste being a part of the earth's nutrient cycle, we take so many toxins into our bodies that the waste itself has become toxic. Again we are moved from the cycles of the farm and into the patterns of a mine where value is extracted to never be returned.

Limitless Consequences

Our economic and political life thrives in this denial of limits, carnal and ecological, because the further we can move from the realities of the physical, the realities of the Real, the greater are the possibilities for desire to grow and thrive. It is the limitless exercise of desire that enables capitalist society to work. Limits don't sell. Limits enable us to see the contours of our life for what they are and to learn the satisfactions of living in reality. If you watch TV (and if you don't, God bless you) pay attention one evening to how many times advertisements mention limitlessness as a selling point—limitless possibilities, limitless miles, etc. The escape from limits has been the human temptation since the Garden of Eden and it has always been predicated upon an escape from reality.

This escape has, over time, been managed by a millennia spanning cooking of the books. Take soil, which the agrarians would remind us is our most basic of dependencies. Civilization after civilization has built itself, utilizing grain as the base of its agriculture. And yet grain has always required large spaces cultivated with one crop, creating the opportunity for massive crop failures, erosion, and eventually soil nutrient depletion. The growing of large scale grain crops has relied on a mining of nutrients laid over millennia by soil nourishing ecosystems and geological formations such as forests or glacial deposits. In modern agriculture the life of these soils has been extended by synthetic fertilizers that work to nourish plants, but not soils, leaving the dirt, the ground from which we were formed, even more depleted.

Our escape from limits takes a multitude of other forms as well. For example there is the driving of cars, a form of transportation for which we're willing to sacrifice one life every thirteen minutes in the name of speed. The freeway is a perfect representation of our desire to escape from limits and its consequences—it is the path for speed far beyond a human pace, and with that speed we have seen the destructive work of sprawl on our cities and countryside. As Jane Jacobs has said, "Not TV or illegal drugs but the automobile has been the chief destroyer of American communities."[2]

Another modern metaphor for a life lived against limits is the vampire. In the wonderful "B" movie *The Addiction*, a philosophy PhD candidate is infected by a vampire. As she grows in her new identity, she appears healthy on the outside, more powerful than ever, but discovers that her body is rotting and decaying from the inside. It is not dissimilar in our life—personal, social, bodily, economic. In denial of our basic dependencies—our creatureliness which give us purpose, meaning and limits—we are dying from the inside. Yet in many ways the exterior of our lives does not reflect the wasteland inside. We are rotting, but no one knows.

We hide and externalize our destruction to places where people of privilege cannot see it—places on the margins whether it is the inner city or the rural countryside. This is the basic structure of imperial existence—it relies on the slavery of a whole network of provinces to feed the power and success of the imperial center.

2. Jacobs, *Dark Age*, 37.

Most urban dwellers are unaware of the assault on the countryside that has been happening over the last fifty-odd years across the globe. This now includes the export of trash from cities to rural places or from rich countries to poor ones. Much of Europe's trash, for instance, is sent to West Africa; New York's to rural Ohio. From nuclear waste to prisons, the "refuse" of industrial civilization is put out of sight.

In her wonderful essay, "Wilderness," Marilynn Robinson writes that "Wilderness is where things can be done that would be intolerable in a populous landscape. The relative absence of human populations obscures the nature and effect of programs which have no other object than to be capable of the most profound injury to human populations."[3] We need wilderness in a society that seeks to escape its limits in order to have some place, out there, to hide our deficits and bear our debts. Robinson suggests that we give up the idea of wilderness, and "accept the fact that the consequences of human presence in the world are universal and ineluctable."[4] It is only through seeing the whole of our connections that we can begin to come to terms with our limits, and live within the discipline of their consequences.

Disciplines of Dependence

To answer the discipline of our limits, to accept them as a gift rather than a curse, we must embrace practices that help us understand our dependence. We can begin by slowing down our lives. This is a critical first step because it is easy to begin another long list of must-dos, of things that we have to accomplish. In this situation we are at risk of finding ourselves busily connecting with the land, gardening, resisting consumer economy at a rate that outstrips our limitations of skill and health. So it is essential that we begin with a clearing, a slowing down.

This slowing down is helped with the development of a Sabbath practice—the first discipline of dependence. To spend one day

3. Robinson, *Death of Adam*, 247.
4. Ibid., 254.

free from money, from work, from planned activities—even at best without driving anywhere—this is the kind of practice we need to learn the gift and joy of dependence. It is a celebration of being—which is essentially what the gift of dependence is all about. We are not what we produce, we are not what we make, we are not what we do—we simply are. Our meaning is defined by our Creator, so we can relax.

Through the disciplines we gain through practicing the Sabbath well, we can carry over slowness into the other aspects of our lives as well. The Sabbath teaches us the discipline of the no that is yes—how to sacrifice activity for being. When we truly embrace the wonder and goodness of being we will find ourselves seeking small Sabbaths throughout the day—times of delight without any other purpose. These Sabbaths are not to rejuvenate us to work harder or longer; their only purpose is to delight in the goodness of being. The Sabbath will also train us to easily make our way into longer retreats.

In my own struggle to Sabbath, my priest and spiritual director Father Ed reminded me that in order to take a longer spiritual retreat one must first practice the Sabbath and that in order to practice the Sabbath we must learn to have moments of solitude and being throughout the week. The celebration of Sabbath is a skill, delight takes practice.

To find delight in the Sabbath—a day that is always a feast, we must also learn to fast. Fasting enables us to say no—it too is an important form of slowness and a way of deeply embracing our dependence. Fasting for Christians is always done with an understanding that we do not live on bread alone. This is a statement that the fundamental sources of our life are not biological, but divine. As Psalm 104:27–30 teaches us:

> These all look to you to give them their food in due season;
>
> when you give to them, they gather it up; when you open your hand, they are filled with good things.
>
> When you hide your face, they are dismayed; when you take away their breath, they die and return to their dust.

When you send forth your spirit, they are created; and you
renew the face of the ground.

When we fast we are deciding to live in the acknowledgement of
our dependence—it puts us into a state of frailty and humility. But
fasting can also be an act of strength—a way of training our will.
The ability to fast, to resist something that we want in favor of a
greater good, is an essential skill, not only for holiness but responsibility. Let's take meat. Many people believe that it is wrong to eat
the meat of animals that were raised and slaughtered in inhumane
conditions. Yet many continue to eat meat because they simply can't
resist the urge. With fasting we are given the ability to say no, I'll
wait for something better.

To wait for something better—that is an important place for
us to live as Christ's followers in an age that would offer us many
things "now." It is wrong to say that desire should merely be stifled
or disciplined—desire, in the Christian understanding, should be
cultivated. It must be grown and developed toward the right end
and we must be willing to sacrifice the cheap and counterfeit offers of fulfilling that desire. In fasting we not only acknowledge that
food is not our sole source of life, but we also bear witness to a
hunger that is deeper than the hunger for food. This is a hunger for
God, for God's kingdom and righteousness. It is in the satisfaction
of that hunger that we will be actualized as human beings.

With these two disciplines, fasting and Sabbath, we are
brought closer to our understanding of who we are as people who
receive our life as a gift. And when we begin to understand our
lives as given, limited, and dependent, we come to understanding
that we live on the creature side of the creation—that we are not
the masters of creation, or even its stewards. Our vocation is for
something else.

Creatures not Stewards

Kelly Johnson, in her wonderful book *The Fear of Beggars*, offers
a critique of the stewardship ethic that is worth considering here,
particularly since it reorients our position to the side of the gift

rather than the giver. Johnson writes that stewardship "requires no disruption of social structures, endows no romantic spiritual excellence on the poor, leaves the order of property rights largely uncontested."[5] The language of stewardship, Johnson points out, even found its way into antebellum Southern discussions of slavery, with slave owners claiming a "sacred trust" that they had in the care and keep of their slaves.

This last history of the use of "stewardship" should give us particular pause because it points to the most disastrous possibilities for an environmental stewardship ethic. If we are stewards of the land we are given the managerial tasks of deciding how to use resources with considerations, like any good manager of risks and benefits, costs and profits. We might be tempted to think that the destruction of *this* mountain in order to get coal would be a worthwhile trade off for the greater good of the energy provided. But if we do not see ourselves as stewards, as the managers of creation, but instead see ourselves as merely creatures within the creation, such moves would be pure acts of hubris for which we would be held accountable. We would certainly think this of the slave owner claiming stewardship over a fellow human being. Why not think the same of the "steward of creation"?

We have received the gift of creation, a gift that we are a part of, but it is not we who are its primary caretakers or sustainers. The vocation given to Adam in Genesis 2 was not that of steward, but rather of servant to the garden and its soil—employee rather than manager. To truly understand our role we must read Genesis 1:28–30 while also reading Genesis 2:15–17. In Genesis 1:28–30 humankind is given dominion, but in Genesis 2:15–17 humankind is given a vocation, or purpose to its dominion, to "keep the garden." And within that vocation humankind is also given a limit, we are to enjoy the abundance of the garden, but it is not all ours to do with what we please. When we read both passages together it becomes problematic to see the human role as purely that of the steward.

Perhaps a better metaphor for our role in creation would be that of priest or minister. Following Stanley Hauerwas and John

5. Johnson, *Beggars*, 99.

Berkman, we might say that our role within creation is to remind creation of its purpose and story:

> To put it most simply, the only significant theological dif-
> ference between humans and animals lies in God's giv-
> ing humans a unique *purpose*. Herein lies what it means
> for God to create humans in God's image. A part of this
> unique purpose is God's charge to humans to tell animals
> who they are, and humans continue to do this by the very
> way they relate to other animals. We think there is an
> analogous relationship here: animals need humans to tell
> them their story, just as gentiles need Jews to tell them
> their story.[6]

We are given perhaps our best picture of human dependence within creation and our proper vocation in the book of Job. When God appears to Job in the whirlwind, he doesn't call Job's attention to the vast expanses of creation that are under Job's stewardship, but rather to the wide array of creation that is completely unknown and inaccessible to the would-be steward. See these verses from Job 38:4–7, 39–41:

> Where were you when I laid the foundation of the earth?
> Tell me, if you have understanding.
> Who determined its measurements—surely you know!
> Or who stretched the line upon it?
> On what were its bases sunk, or who laid its cornerstone
> when the morning stars sang together
> and all the heavenly beings shouted for joy?. . .
> "Can you hunt the prey for the lion,
> or satisfy the appetite of the young lions,
> when they crouch in their dens,
> or lie in wait in their covert?
> Who provides for the raven its prey,
> when its young ones cry to God,
> and wander about for lack of food?

---

6. Hauerwas and Berkman, "Chief End," 199.

God is clearly the master of creation and Job is no more than one part of it—steward hardly fits the image.

In a world of vast technology, thousands of centers of learning and research, and an ever increased ability to share information, we are still discovering new species of animals, and not only animals in the remote reaches of the deep sea (where organisms are being discovered that defy what we thought possible for life, including bacteria that eat about once a century), but also animals as commonplace as birds. To be the stewards of such a world we would have to be fairly ignorant managers of the estate of creation.

In the biblical account Job is described as being brought to "repent in dust and ashes" by God's reply. This is an appropriate response and one that recalls us not to the pretense of stewardship, but the vocation of humility. To be humble, as Bernard of Clairvaux has taught us, is to live in the truth.[7] When God responds to Job he is bringing Job into the truth and Job's response is to be brought back to the earth—to dust and ashes. This process we call humiliation. We are *adam* from *adamah*, human from humus—to be humbled is to be returned and reminded that we are but soil. To be soil is to be lowly but it is not to be lifeless—dust and ashes, these are the source of life for flora and fauna alike. We are people of the dust, called from the dust, to serve it. What if instead of stewards we became servants of the soil—farmers in the best sense? What would that look like?

An exemplar that comes to mind is Will Allen, the founder of Growing Power, an organization that has been growing amazing amounts of food in urban places for several decades. Allen talks about soil as the bedrock of any garden and so he has dedicated himself to developing soil. Allen composts huge amounts of would-be waste, seeing the problems of others as an amazing gift. Allen also raises earthworms by the millions—the worms working in the soil to turn vegetable waste and brewers grains, plentiful in Allen's native Milwaukee, into rich dark soil. This work, of making good soil, is as close as I can imagine the human vocation in Eden. To make compost—that is true service to the soil.

7. Bernard, *Humility*, 29.

The result of this attention to the soil is the unleashing of God's abundance. As Will Allen frequently says, "Pay attention to the soil and you can grow anything." Agrarian and contrary farmer Gene Logsdon makes the claim that the work of building good soil is as great as any other human pursuit: "If your gravestone could read, 'Here lies a person who left his land with over 5 percent organic matter in it,' you could rest assured that you had contributed as much good to the earth as any famed scientist, philosopher, or philanthropist. Maybe more."[8]

A life lived within the limits of our purpose, within the limits of our biology and scale, within the limits of our understanding is a good life. It is a life that is true to the reality of what and who we are as people. Our limits are a gift, just as our life is a gift—born from the God who is love and is therefore fecund since love is always an expanding circle—the source of birth.

One important part of the revolution of Jesus was to remind us that God is our Father. This means that we are a part of a family, a household. In this family we are invited into a loving existence where we are able to simply be—to exist as my daughter Lily exists. She can do nothing, she has no way to earn her keep, she has little to offer. She is dependent, radically limited, and loved because she exists. That is what a gift is—a radical existence that has escaped exchange, the constant human desire to place wealth within a market. A gift is given outside of calculation, in a way where "our left hand doesn't know what our right is doing." Its value is weighed and measured in heaven, where it is stored, keeping it a gift that cannot be turned into an item of exchange.

Unfortunately, we live in a world that has denied gifts of all kinds, especially the gift of dependence. We have forgotten that we have a Father who provides, a Father who gives beyond exchange. Like bastard children we think we must earn our love and our purpose, that we must make meaningful and useful what is good in and of itself. It is time to rediscover our home and our family, to learn that our meals will come, our good will be provided for. These are things we must learn to receive. I have a priest friend who

8. Logsdon, *Soil*, 3

says that there are many in his congregation who simply can't hold out their hand and receive the bread—they must take it. Reception requires the humility that reality is always ready to provide through the painful process of being brought low. Love is ready when we are.

3

Commonwealths

"As soon as the land of any country has all become
private property, the landlords, like all other men,
love to reap where they never sowed, and demand a
rent even for its natural produce."
—ADAM SMITH

If creation is a gift and we are given, then we must ask, what does
ownership mean? How can one have property, belongings, titles,
and deeds, when everything is a gift? The answer is not easy. No-
madic American Indians, when they first came across white set-
tlers, were incredulous at the idea of land ownership—an idea they
considered as absurd as owning the sky. And yet land rights are
certainly older than European understandings of property. We see
discussions of property rights littered throughout the Bible from
Abraham to Naboth and his vineyard. Yet even in the Christian
tradition, an understanding of how we view property has not been
easy, particularly when Christ and early Christians seem to have
held personal property ownership in low regard.

The way that the tensions of property ownership have been
resolved for the most part, as articulated by Kelly Johnson in *The
Fear of Beggars*, is the idea that the gift of creation must be answered
with a sense of responsibility for that gift—that we must come to see

ourselves as stewards of the land. Ownership then becomes a means of greater responsibility; as the argument goes, "I will take care of what I own." This idea that ownership and responsibility go hand in hand has become so pervasive in our culture that we even think that it is important for us to "own" our faith.

John Locke, one of the Enlightenment's foundational thinkers and a particularly influential thinker on the founders of the United States, was well aware of the difficulty of formulating property rights if creation is a gift: "God, as king David says, Psal CXV 16, *has given the earth to the children of men*; given it to mankind in common. But this being supposed, it seems to some a very great difficulty, how any one should ever come to have a *property* in any thing" (emphasis his).[1]

The way Locke solves this problem in his *Second Treatise of Government* is by arguing that each person is property to him or herself, and that it is through mixing one's labor with a part of the commonwealth that one becomes its owner:

> Though the Earth, and all inferior Creatures be common to all Men, yet every Man has a *Property* in his own *Person*. This no Body had any Right to but himself. The *Labour* of his Body, and the *Work* of his Hands, we may say, are properly his. Whatsoever then he removes out of the State that Nature hath provided, and left it in, he hath mixed his *Labour* with, and joyned to it something that is his own, and thereby makes it his *Property*. It being by him removed from the common state Nature placed it in, it hath by this *labour* something annexed to it, that excludes the common right of other Men. For this *Labour* being the unquestionable Property of the Labourer, no Man but he can have a right to what that is once joyned to, at least where there is enough, and as good left in common for others.[2]

For instance, if someone goes into a common forest, like a state Wildlife Management Area, and shoots a deer, then that deer will properly be the hunter's. But where Locke really begins to articulate

1. Locke, *Government*, 208.
2. Ibid., 209–10.

his unique position comes later in the treatise when he seeks to articulate how value relates to property, and where value is properly located. Creation, Locke argues, is essentially valueless—a raw material—until it becomes mixed up with human labor:

> God gave the world to men in common; but since he gave it for their benefit, and the greatest conveniences of life they were capable to draw from it, it cannot be supposed he meant it should always remain common and uncultivated. He gave it to the use of the industrious and rational, (and *labour* was to be *his title* to it); not to the fancy or covetousness of the quarrelsome and contentious.[3]

In other words God gave the world as a raw material to be made valuable by English Protestants. The creation in itself is valueless, but by *improving it* we make it valuable and therefore can claim it as property because the value we have given to the land is then mixed up with it.

Locke goes on to show how, through buying something, our labor is mixed with it, thereby making our ownership legitimate— the purchase of something is a mixing of value with the raw materials of creation. We then no longer have to till the land in order to have a claim to it, we must simply have labored by another means in order to gain money and then transfer that labor and its value to the tilled land.

This articulation of property rights is clearly brilliant and has certainly been influential, but Locke's view has many flaws that have resulted in the destructive use of property as a means to limit and diminish the abundant gifts of God. It is our task now to parse out how exactly Locke's view limits our ability to embrace the abundance of God. We must then ask how we might recover a different understanding of our relationship to the gifts of creation outside of the property paradigm.

3. Ibid., 214.

The Body

The basis of Locke's understanding of property relies on his idea that the body is our primary property—the foundation from which all other property arises: "Though the Earth, and all inferior Creatures be common to all Men, yet every Man has a *Property* in his own *Person*. This no Body had any Right to but himself."[4]

As we can see from the preceding chapter, our dependencies alone would make this claim of our own persons being property to ourselves questionable. But it is not only our dependencies, but also our dependents that make our bodies commonwealths more than private possessions—our bodies are centers of life on which many others have legitimate claims.

When my daughter was born and my wife Emily and I began discovering what Donald Rumsfield would call "unknown unknowns," among them was our daughter's absolutely radical dependence. This may seem obvious and of course we knew that she would be dependent upon us, but the fact that she could not even hold her head up and can hardly articulate her wants or needs, even through a cry, is something difficult to fully grasp until one has experienced a newborn.

It seems that this other side of dependence, to be depended upon, is as challenging in late capitalist society as being dependent. To be depended upon shows radically how our lives are not singular, how our bodies are not individual. Take abortion, which is centrally the mechanical destruction of dependence. So much of the abortion debate, on both sides, has focused on the rights of the mother or the rights of the unborn child over their bodies (rights language born from Enlightenment thinkers like Locke). But this rights language significantly diminishes the human person and does not address the reality of pregnancy or birth. A woman's body is not her own, an infant's body is not her own, and let us be clear to add that a man's body is not his own—they are interconnected in a network of

4. Ibid., 209.

gifts—internal and external to the body. The human person is not private property; in other words, it is a commonwealth.

We fear commonwealths in large part because they require cooperation more than control; they mean that others may have a claim on the same goods we do. We want to control the demands and requirements of our life, we want to control the use and disuse of our goods, but when we must cooperate with others around such things it requires more work, it requires compromise and sacrifice, it requires most of all slowness.

To be a member of a commonwealth means that we must be response-able—this is the primary requirement of the depended upon. To be responsible requires that we open ourselves to the cry of those outside of ourselves—that we must open ourselves to "give to those who ask" when they ask. It means also that we must accept and cultivate our "abilities" so that we can make a good response when called upon. To be a part of this *whole* we must sacrifice an aspect of our *part*—we must give over our independence.

To be independent is impossible of course, but to live in that illusion we must find ways to alienate and ignore our dependencies. We must also give up our place in the network of dependencies by relieving ourselves of the work that would put us into contact with them. This requires a master-slave relationship in which we subjugate others to our needs by denying the legitimacy of their own call.

In one of the most provocative passages of Wendell Berry's classic work, *The Unsettling of America*, Berry makes this point boldly:

> We have made it our overriding ambition to escape work, and as a consequence have debased work until it is only fit to escape from . . . Out of this contempt for work arose the idea of a nigger: at first some person, and later some thing, to be used to relieve us of the burden of work. If we began by making niggers of people, we have ended by making a nigger of the world . . . We have made of the rivers and oceans and winds niggers to carry away our refuse, which we think we are too good to dispose of decently ourselves. And in doing this to the world that is our common heritage and bond, we have returned to

> making niggers of people: we have become each other's
> niggers.[5]

As Berry articulates with disruptive offensiveness, we can live comfortably in an economy abounding in cheap consumer goods only because we have objectified the people and places that make those goods possible. We have denied the commonwealths of land, air, and water, turning them into the private goods of profit and exploitation; no matter the cost to us all—which is where the true costs lie. It is no wonder then that without the commonwealth of places we would deny the commonwealth of people and the commonwealth of our bodies.

Members Not Owners

If we deny Locke's idea that our bodies are property—and thus things that might be rented out or sold—then we are able to begin the dismantling of his whole conception of ownership. If our bodies and lives are a gift, working in concert with the gift of creation and the gift of other lives, then how do we describe that reality as it pertains to the goods of life that Locke tries to help us own?

The agrarian response is that we are members. Being members means that we do not work effectively alone and do not exist coherently alone—we are a part of a larger whole and it is through working well within that whole that we attain our own good, which is always in harmony with the good of the whole. To be a member means that we are a gift to each other and our work and lives may be judged according to how well we have lived out that call of gift.

Membership requires dues, it requires responsibility and agreement to a common set of rules. Take a membership in a country club (to pick a deeply un-agrarian example). To be a member of a country club requires that one pays for the honor, but payment is often not enough. There is also the requirement of a contract; certain rules must be followed, such as a dress code. Many clubs also require that members join only through a selection process

5. Berry, *Unsettling*, 12.

controlled by other members—that is in part what makes membership desirable, because it is exclusive it means something.

Or take another example, one I'm a bit more personally familiar with—a hunting club. Many hunters belong to clubs that lease land and manage it for wildlife. To be a part of the club one must usually do some work to set up the hunting camp, tend to the wildlife food plots, or create and maintain wildlife habitat. Someone who acts recklessly or doesn't fulfill their responsibility of participation wouldn't be allowed back in most clubs. The club exists around the common sharing of resources and so it is critical that those resources be respected by all who are members.

To be a part of a commonwealth requires membership—the more conscious we are of this reality the better able we are to serve our role as members. But of course we don't always choose our membership—we live or are born into them. Part of growing up is learning the rules and responsibilities of our memberships. Watersheds serve as a clear example of this form of membership. To share in the common resource of Lake Maumelle one must simply live in Little Rock, Arkansas. Drink any water from the tap and it comes from this lake. But when this particular watershed was threatened by developers wanting to build along its shores, surprisingly few people, other than dedicated environmentalists, showed up to oppose the development. The managers of the watershed are faced with a constant effort to get people to pay attention to this basic good provided to Little Rock residents—a good that doesn't come without a great deal of management and vigilance.

Owning the Commonwealth

To be a part of a commonwealth does not exclude the rights and responsibilities of individuals, families, or communities—instead commonwealths work to preserve those rights and responsibilities against the amorphous powers of monopolistic institutions such as the State and corporations.

In this way, people who are owners of land, such as farmers and ranchers, play an important role in protecting it. But key to this protection is an understanding on the owner's part that this land for which they are responsible is a part of a greater whole.

As I write, there is a major debate raging about the creation of a pipeline from the Canadian Tarsands to refineries in the Gulf. Some of the greatest opponents of the pipeline are ranchers in Nebraska who not only want to keep the pipeline off their land, but also want to protect the huge and critical Ogallala aquifer. Randy Thompson, one rancher who has led the fight against the pipeline, talks about how hard his parents worked through the Depression to hold on to the land that has served as his family's livelihood for generations. "I know what my folks went through to get a piece of ground. And these sons of bitches come along and they tell me 'we're going to take this land away from you whether you want us to or not,'" he says, "and they got a fight on their hands."

In this conflict over the protection of land, and the use of immanent domain to take it for a pipeline, we see essentially two kinds of ownership in conflict. There is ownership of the kind that Transcanada claims—essentially the rights of conquest, where each particular place is only a dot on a highway and of no consequence but for the pipeline that passes through it. And then there is the ownership of the land by Randy Thompson, who feels a responsibility for this particular land because he knows the place and its history.

Belonging

Agrarianism points us not to some communistic common ownership, but rather to democratic ownership—ownership that considers the whole, the democracy of the dead, the common concerns of all. Randy Thompson sees his time on the land he owns as a moment in a continuum that is attached to the lives of many others who have also been responsible for the land—his parents who purchased the land first and his children who will work the land after him. In his ownership of this one piece of land he recognizes that the borders of his responsibility extend beyond his land and that the borders of his neighbor's responsibility extend within his fences.

For TransCanada, Randy Thompson's land is simply a property line that fell within the route their Geographic Information Specialists plotted as the best path for their pipeline. The oil they want to transport through that pipeline also comes from land that has no value to TransCanada as a place. Places are only the sites of profit and conquest for such a company, "trans" being the operative description in its name. The oil itself, transported over all those places of inconsequence, has no value except within a market centered on the abstract exchange of money. In the end TransCanada's pipeline will exist, for the moment it operates along its path from Canada to the Gulf, without *belonging*.

"Belong" comes from the Old English *langian*, which means, to pertain to, go along with—to belong in other words requires a certain fittingness. If I belong to a place I fit there, I become a part of it. A pipeline doesn't belong on Randy Thompson's land—it doesn't fit there. TransCanada doesn't belong on the tundra where it leaves vast scars in the land as it extracts tar sands oil. To belong means to fit and to fit requires a certain ecological democracy—we must be a part of a whole in a way that promotes the common good of all. Belonging requires the tacit vote of the other members of the commonwealth before we can properly say we ourselves are members.

TransCanada cannot be a member because it does not belong—it relies on hegemony and monopoly to seek its goods rather than cooperation and mutual aid. It is telling that as soon as people like Randy Thompson refused to accept payment for the right of easement across their land TransCanada immediately began sending threatening letters, attempting to utilize the power of the State (which in some cases they did not have). Persuasion, the tool of membership and participation, was quickly abandoned because of the monopolistic nature of TransCanada's good. All they have to offer is money and after that is refused, there is nothing left for them to do but to take the land through immanent domain—the violent take it by force.

Re-Membering the Body

Ownership in the agrarian habit of mind requires membership. Like a neighborhood association of the world, our ownership is not absolute but contingent—and this applies to our bodies as much as our land. In fact as we have seen from our reading of Locke, the argument for an absolute right to property is dependent upon the assumption of an absolute right to one's own person.

It is here that agrarianism again has something critical to remind the church. It is the church that helps us see that when we are fully human we are members of a body, not bodies unto ourselves. And yet this is a reality many churches have forgotten, choosing instead to be dominated by the property mindset of a consumer society. In my own city, there is a choose-your-own-adventure kind of church—a place where church members are given, each Sunday, the option of a community in which they would like to be a part. If you are a fan of praise music, then New Community is for you; if you are a rocker who wants electric guitars in your worship, then the Edge is your place. If you just want the plain old regular service you can attend that as well.

When properly formed a church is a place where we don't come to be divided according to our psychographics and demographics. The church properly formed is a place where we come to *re-member*. In each weekly gathering we read from the scriptures, join in the common act of worship, and most importantly remember the breaking of Christ's body which allows us to become a part of the body of God.

The most comprehensive passage on this remembering is of course 1 Corinithians 12—Paul's great statement on the church as Christ's body. It would be helpful for us, in working toward an understanding of what we should do with the gifts of creation, to look more deeply at this passage.

The passage begins, first of all, addressing the question of gifts. These are gifts of the Spirit, but I think that we can read the passage more broadly with an eye to understand how we should relate to all of the gifts of God.

Paul begins interestingly by reminding the Corinthian church of their lack of understanding prior to their conversion. As a group of pagan converts they had once worshiped idols that Paul notes were mute—unable to speak. He then tells the Corinthians that truthful speech, speech that properly acknowledges Christ as lord, can only exist when one is given that speech through the Holy Spirit. The pagan gods cannot speak at all, but a Christian cannot speak unless prompted to do so by the Holy Spirit.

Paul then states that the Spirit gives many different kinds of gifts—parts of a sort of ecclesial ecosystem. Just as in a commonwealth, the commons are not healthy without a diversity of goods, so a church is not healthy without the varied gifts of its members. Paul tells us that each one of these gifts, which are manifestations of the Spirit, "are for the common good."

What is given to one, one's property or skill or talent, we might say, is for the common good—it must always be seen, according to Paul, as part of a collective good that is larger than any single part.

Paul then moves into his primary metaphor—the body. The body of Christ, the church that Paul describes, is made up of a multitude of parts that must work in concert and harmony for the whole to be healthy. We are dependent on each part working, however lowly—each part is necessary. If Paul were writing today, he could easily have used the metaphor of ecology—another system in which each part works toward the health of the whole. For instance a healthy grassland cannot exist without the interaction of heavy animals like elephants and buffalo. And these large animals require the interaction of smaller animals, like dung beetles which roll the large animals' manure into small pellets, and bury them in the ground which in turn fertilizes the grass. For the kingdom of God to work we must have the dung beetles and the elephants—it is a mistake of valuation to place one above the other. As E. O. Wilson has said, the world's ecosystems can function just fine without human presence, but they cannot do so without ants. While agrarians would not completely agree, the point still holds true—lowly ants are just as important if not more so than the most "advanced" animal on the planet.

The key to this body, this ecosystem, this membership, is love. And it is love that Paul turns to just following this passage in 1 Corinthians 13. It is love that binds the gift of the body into one. It is love that must be the center of any economy that seeks the common good. It is through love that we are re-membered.

An Economy of Agape

If our lives were animated by love as articulated in 1 Corinthians 13, if we did not envy, were not proud, did not dishonor others or seek our own, if we did not keep a tally of wrongs, but always sought to live in the truth, and trust, hope, and persevere toward the common good, how would property, my border against your border, make sense? A community of agape is a community in which love is the greatest, immeasurable measurement of health.

Think of Randy Thompson and TransCanada. TransCanada wants a pipeline so that they can refine more oil, sell more gasoline, and there are some who say we need that. And yet the goods of a pipeline are always at the expense of others, whether it is Randy Thompson's land or the aquifer beneath it. To describe love as the guide to TransCanada's actions is clearly absurd.

So we must ask, what wealth is there outside of the common-wealth, outside of love? A Bishop from Congo came to deliver the homily at a church I was member of several years ago, and in his sermon he expressed the great need for faith among his people because they had nothing else. "We pray for healing because we have no alternative but to pray, and yet we often see our prayers answered," he said. For Americans, however, he said "that since we have so much in material wealth we feel like we need nothing from God." We do not become wealthy in a simple way—wealth without love, without proper form, easily becomes poverty of another kind.

If we want to truly understand the wealth that might come from an enterprise such as the TransCanada pipeline with its potential to create jobs and lower oil prices, we must also ask what kind of poverty it will create. If we evaluate the wealth to be created from a truly democratic perspective, a perspective that takes into consideration all of the voices that will be affected—the creatures on the land, the generations to come, the people who rely on a secure and safe aquifer for water—then such an enterprise would be difficult to appraise as a clear "wealth" creating enterprise. Rather than wealth, it is likely to only create money for a few.

Celebrating the Commonwele

One cannot have wealth without health. The two words are linked by etymology and meaning. The word *wealth* is derived from the Middle English word *wele* which refers to well-being. To be wealthy is to have well-being. It is only through a plutocentric and consumerist culture that we have come to equate wealth with money, though no doubt resources can play a role in well-being. But as Wendell Berry and Wes Jackson articulated, money is too small a measure to articulate a standard for the *commonwele*—the common well-being.

So how should we find a better standard? Perhaps one question we might ask is, "can we celebrate it?" Can we imagine an annual pipeline celebration? Would that make sense? Can we have an annual celebration of oil executives? It seems absurd, but the same does not seem absurd when we think of farming and farmers, or any number of crafts and craftsmen. Many cultures have ways of celebrating the harvest and other forms of good work that serve the common wealth.

Real wealth—wealth that is attached to health, can be easily marked by a public celebration of the goods contained within the commons. This is a frequent theme in Wendell Berry's fiction, particularly his portrayals of bygone times. Common work and labor are combined with celebration, sometimes to hilarious effect as in the story "Don't Send a Body to Do a Man's Work," where a hog killing celebration gets out of hand as moonshine begins to flow in the fictional community of Port William. Dances, socials, harvest festivals—these are common features of Berry's stories and they are true to the life of the communities Port William reflects.

Modern echoes of this can be found in some of the Amish communities of Pennsylvania and Ohio around the common work of threshing or barn-raising. Threshing is a labor intensive process through which grain is harvested, dried and then separated from the chaff. It is hard work, and takes a good number of people to make effective work of it by hand. Most modern, industrial farms now use machines to do the work, but many Amish communities still do the work manually.

This collective manual work means that neighbors must come together over a series of days, moving from farm to farm, day after day. The men do the threshing and the women cook big meals each day to feed everyone. Each day the threshing work is a celebration where good work is done and a community is re-membered. Many Amish communities, however, have opted to adopt modern threshing machines to save themselves from the hard work of threshing. David Kline, an Amish bishop, farmer, and writer, has observed that in Amish church communities that have decided to move to machine threshing there is a marked decline in the community life of those churches. Without the common work toward the common good, celebration is then isolated to special occasions rather than a climax of daily life. Just consider what has happened to harvest festivals in many places in America—they are hardly tied to the real work of harvest. Instead, most harvest fests are simply alternatives to Halloween—a holiday that has also lost its roots by being divorced, in most contexts, from All Saints Day.

The disappearance of the commons has meant not only a lack of celebration, but also its privatization. This has become particularly true in the church where family celebrations of critical Christian holidays like Easter and Christmas trump parish celebrations of these holidays. My wife and I wrestled with this question when we had to address the baptism of our daughter. The most obvious time for her to be baptized, according to church tradition, would have been at the Easter vigil. And yet, that was a day that did not work for many family members to attend. We wrestled with the question of whether we should choose a day that is powerfully representative of the resurrection of which baptism is a symbol or whether we should choose a day when our family could all join us.

We decided that since the purpose of baptism is to move from the bond of blood to water, it was fitting that we should choose the date around the ecclesial calendar rather than the family one, but it was a difficult decision with a great deal of tension involved.

If we are to restore our commonwealths then perhaps our first move should be in celebrating those things we already share. Imagine a watershed festival in which a city celebrates the lake that provides fresh water. Harvest festivals must be restored as real celebrations of the abundance God has provided, rather than Halloween alternatives. The church has a critical role to play in this because we have retained, more than other parts of society, the ability to celebrate collectively. The recovery of Rogation days as real requests to God for the blessing of crops would be an excellent first step for churches.

Conclusion

John Locke created his theory of property, rooted in the right to our own person, to protect mine from yours in a world where scarcity dominates. But in a world where God's gifts are abundant, unlocked in our common work toward the common good, we don't need the same kind of relationship with property. Instead, through neighbor helping neighbor, each working for what is good for all, we can find a way beyond Lockeian property to a commonwealth in which we all participate. Our ownership is transferred from our right to our history—the tradition of our participation in a place and our work toward its common good rather than an abstract claim. We are members of one another, one with another—and this membership changes our ownership from our bodies to the land of which they are a part.

4

A Body of Earth

"If anything is sacred, the human body is sacred."
—WALT WHITMAN

The economy of unreality—the economy of the strip mine and the interstate, the drive-through restaurant and the drive-through pharmacy—has been marked by an assault on the body. This assault started with a separation, like any good military strategy the body was first isolated before it was destroyed. It was isolated—first from the land, then from the soul, and finally from itself.

The body was isolated from the land when it no longer lived in partnership and at the mercy of the creation. "At the mercy of"— consider how that phrase now strikes us. It is a scary proposition, one filled with uncertainty, and yet our only option other than living at the mercy of creation is to live under the cruelty of nature. We have lost the ability to know the difference because we have been a people who live and die "insured" and isolated.

Agriculture itself was a kind of insurance that quickly moved to isolate us from both instinct and the creation at whose mercy we lived. For most of human history we lived in a cooperative dance with the creation, hunting and gathering. We were not simply passive in this activity, but from all of the meager evidence of pre-history it appears that we were active participants in the encouraging of a flourishing creation. Hunters would spread seeds and develop habitats that would encourage a diversity of game at easy reach. It is likely that through some of these activities the domestication of sheep came about—the first domesticated animals.

The great divide between people and the land came when grains were developed on a large scale in Mesopotamia. The human diet became less varied at the same time that civilization or "city life" grew and developed. The grains, grown on a large scale, provided a ready source of sustenance, but not a healthy source of nutrition. The small garden plots of hunter-gathers gave way to large scale agriculture which required large scale land clearing and the replacement of varied flora with monocultures. The soil, no longer tied into the cycles of nutrient exchange, began to suffer and the cycle of the rise and fall of civilizations began. The certainty of large scale agriculture then began to create what is always the inevitable result of insurance, more radical uncertainty. As we increased a storable resource, we did so through an accumulation of ecological debts that eventually, however long they may be deferred, come to bear.[1]

With the rise of large scale grain-based agriculture came not only the destruction of the soil, but also the introduction of new diseases of civilization—heart disease, gout, new forms of cancer. These were the result of a decreased variety of food in the diet and toxins in many Neolithic foods. Many cereal grains for instance contain lectins, a protective toxin of seeds that can erode the intestinal barrier. Large scale agriculture also led to the depletion of key protective nutrients from the soil such as riboflavin, which is destroyed in the soil when high rates of synthetic nitrogen is introduced.[2]

The move from hunter-gatherer societies, which would be better termed permaculture societies, resulted in a move from cooperative actions within the given world to large scale changes to the creation—including the altering of species through grain development, massive clearing of land, and a serious change in the human diet.

1. For more on the detrimental effects of grain agriculture see *Against the Grain* by Richard Manning.

2. Voison, *Fertilizer Application*, 62–63.

This separation from the land and the move from a dance of partnership with the creation to one of exploitation of natural resources resulted in a removal of the soul from the body. Once the human person was separated from the creation on which it was dependent and of which it was intimately a part, then the natural result was that the body would be left to the earth and the soul would them find its place in a "spiritual realm." The getting of food became more and more a matter of knowledge and management, rather than a sacred gift.

There was a short-lived television show called, "I, Cavemen" in which a group of people were put into a wilderness to live something like primitive hunters and gathers. Using a prehistoric tool called an atlatl to throw a spear—in one scene they successfully kill a caribou. It was remarkable how these modern people reacted to the experience as they rushed over to finish the kill. All of them, even though they were not particularly spiritual, had a kind of sacred experience. They recognized a kind of divine connection in which this life was given so that they may live.

Claudio Oliver has pointed out that the Cain and Abel story may point to a similar break in the experience of the sacred connection with the land. Abel is a keeper of animals, following more closely the pattern of nature, while Cain is a "tiller of the land." As Oliver points out, "It is interesting that *Avad* in Gen 4:2 is in the imperative (accusative) tense, meaning literally to till, instead of only observe or follow nature, but again, work on it, dominate and adapt it, instead of adapt to it."[3] Many commentators have been confused by God's response to Cain's disappointment by God's rejection of his gift: "Why are you disappointed? If you do well, will you not be accepted?" Could it be that God is not pleased with Cain's tilling of the land—his violence against it that then leads to violence against his brother? I find this a more plausible interpretation than simply believing this is a corrupted text as many scholars do.

When the land becomes something that we manage, the body becomes the object of management as well—a temporary material inconvenience that would one day fade to the true "self" inside.

3. Personal correspondence.

With this separation within the "civilized" there came a separation not only of humankind from creation, body from soul, but also physical labor from mental labor. The better off one became, the less work with the physical stuff of the land was necessary. There arose whole underclasses—peasants, slaves, "rednecks" who worked with the physical while the elites, the well off, separated themselves from the physical stuff of life. Even in "health care" where the body is supposedly the central object of work, those who are at the top— doctors, specialists, administrators—work with the body less than those at the bottom—nurses and orderlies who work regularly and directly with the stuff of the body—blood, wounds, urine, feces.

You Should Give a Shit

We may be able to mark the difference between a permaculture society from a society of extraction by how it treats the most basic stuff of animal physicality—shit. Shit, which is etymologically related to shed, meant in its Old English root the excrement of the body. There is no source of shit but the body—it is the stuff that ties us into the network of nutrients that make up the ecosystem in which we live. And yet, we deny shit, we flush it away, treat it, and dispose of it like trash. In doing so we turn the food we eat into a linear process—one of extraction rather than renewal. It doesn't have to be this way.

F. H. King, an agronomist working in the early part of the twentieth century, traveled to Asia to understand the incredible agricultural productivity that Asian farmers had been able to achieve for millennia. What he found was a system of agriculture that took good care of its nutrient cycle. No manure, human or animal, was wasted. It was even considered polite to use the restroom at someone's house before leaving, giving them a little gift for their garden. This was a system that allowed Asia to have a productive agricultural system supporting a large population for forty centuries.[4] As agrarian writer Gene Logsdon notes in his book *Holy Shit: Managing Manure to Save Mankind*, our own system could never last so

4. See F. H. King, *Farmers of Forty Centuries*.

long, "One can only imagine the famine and chaos that would result if we tried to continue that kind of extravagance for forty centuries. As sources of chemical fertilizers decline, either manure will once more become the pot of gold at the end of the rainbow or population levels will dramatically decline."[5]

The denial of shit is at the root of unreality—all illusions begin with the inability to deal with shit. Milan Kundera offers a brilliant analysis of this in his novel *The Unbearable Lightness of Being*. Sabina, a Czech artist in exile in the U.S. goes to a park with a U.S. senator who comments on the beauty of children playing in the grass—"Now, that's what I call happiness." Sabina realizes that part of the senator's reaction to the children is not only at the beauty of the children running on the grass, but also the fact that he was watching this scene with a refugee from a Communist country where, "the senator was convinced, no grass grew or children ran."[6] The senator's sentiment, Sabina realizes, possesses the same aesthetic of a totalitarian. Kundera then launches into a brilliant reflection on what kitsch is:

> Kitsch causes two tears to flow in quick succession. The first tear says: How nice to see children running on the grass!

> The second tear says: How nice to be moved, together with all mankind, by children running on the grass!

> It is the second tear that makes kitsch kitsch.

> The brotherhood of man on earth will be possible only on a base of kitsch.

For Kundera, Kitsch ultimately "is the absolute denial of shit."[7]

The main character of The Unbearable Lightness of Being, Tomás is unable to come to terms with shit and this leaves him unable, ultimately, to believe in the Christian God:

5. Logsdon, *Holy*, 6.

6. Kundera, *Unbearable*, 250.

7. Ibid., 251.

Spontaneously, without any theological training, I, a child, grasped the incompatibility of God and shit and thus came to question the basic thesis of Christian anthropology, namely that man was created in God's image. Either/or: either man was created in God's image—and has intestines!—or God lacks intestines and man is not like him.

The ancient Gnostics felt as I did at the age of five. In the second century, the Great Gnostic master Valentinus resolved the damnable dilemma by claiming that Jesus "ate and drank, but did not defecate."

Shit is a more onerous theological problem than is evil. Since God gave man freedom, we can, if need be, accept the idea that He is not responsible for man's crimes. The responsibility for shit, however, rests entirely with Him, the creator of man.[8]

Against the Gnostics, Christians disciplined by the agrarian mind can say that Christ most certainly shat and that is among the glorious facts of the Incarnation. Christ joined in the great cycles of the creation he spoke into being and it is only in denial, not of Christ's Incarnation, but of our own that this becomes a challenge.

This denial of Christ's shit is at the root of docetism, Gnosticism, and many of the other heresies that have littered Christian history. Tomás is right, if we want to believe in the Christian God we must agree that Christ shitted. The fact that we deny shit means that we would rather live in a world of fantasy, projections of a sanitized world that is readily given to us in a consumer, and especially cyber, culture. If we want to live in and embrace reality then shit must be at the beginning of that—we must worship a God who embraced, and even created, shit. Shit was no part of the fall—our denial is.

What comes from the body connects us again to our source and our limits. This stuff of our body returns to the soil and it is upon the soil that we are dependent. We then live at the mercy of shit.

Ultimately we will shed our entire bodies, flesh mixing with manure as our bodies return to the humus into which God breathed

8. Ibid., 245–46.

life. But just as we deny shit, just as we sanitize and separate and hide away our "soil," we do all we can to keep our bodies from the earth of which they are a part. We have no hope in the body—no hope in its past or its place in the dirt. The body, alienated from its sources, becomes an object separate from the soul that connects us to life. So we seek help, we purchase insurance; we put our trust in the hands of doctors and hospitals and health care systems. All of this enables us to escape the body, to let it be organized and known beyond the mystery that is ourselves.

The Medical Body

The discourse of health care has become hegemonic. Any alternative is met with doubt, and any attempt to opt out foolish. To go without insurance is considered worse than stupid, and yet as soon as we sign on to such plans we begin to be a part of a particular discourse about the body. We are caught, in a desire for the power of medicine and what is the ultimate end of liberalism—a coercion toward a particular good.

As an example, when my wife and I had our daughter Lily, my wife was considered at high risk because of a potential heart condition. We were told that she would have to deliver our daughter in the hospital, in large part because an epidural would be necessary to ensure her heart rate would not climb too high. As it happened, the anesthesiologist, rushing from one place to another, was never able to successfully numb my wife's pain. She essentially had no epidural and the entire reason we were in the hospital was void. In the end we had a good birth experience due to a nurse who played the role of midwife, but her work was hindered by the straps and cords and apparatus of the hospital birth.

As soon as we entered the hospital, my wife's body became the domain of a system, as was my daughter's body when she was born. We had to wait long hours until we were "allowed" to leave and only then after the hospital had approved our car seat. The hospital and the prison, as Foucault articulated, are products of the same discourses of the self.

Wendell Berry, in his classic essay, "Health is Membership," reminds us that what now passes as "health care" is neither health nor care:

> The word "health," in fact, comes from the same Indo-European root as "heal," "whole," and "holy." To be healthy is literally to be whole; to heal is to make whole. I don't think mortal healers should be credited with the power to make holy. But I have no doubt that such healers are properly obliged to acknowledge and respect the holiness embodied in all creatures, or that our healing involves the preservation in us of the spirit and the breath of God.
>
> If we were lucky enough as children to be surrounded by grown-ups who loved us, then our sense of wholeness is not just the sense of completeness in ourselves but also is the sense of belonging to others and to our place; it is an unconscious awareness of community, of having in common. It may be that this double sense of singular integrity and communal belonging is our personal standard of health for as long as we live. Anyhow, we seem to know instinctively that health is not divided.[9]

If we want health care—as we have already said, we must be remembered as people. It is in remembering that the body is restored to its place as a whole—which is in the particular networks of a commonwealth, like a plant in its native ecosystem rather than a pot. To bring things to the right place—that is the proper role of doctoring, a word that has its roots in the latin *docere*—one who makes to appear right, who makes things fit, a teacher.

To heal is to do just this, to make right, to make fit. But medicine all too often doesn't help us fit with reality—to face our death and accept our disease. Medicine doesn't help us to see that death is not unhealthy, a failure of the body, but rather the body's final purpose.

In Berry's story "Fidelity" this reality becomes starkly apparent as Burley Coulter, an old man, sits in a hospital because this was the only possibility offered to his family as a way to care for him.

---

9. Berry, *Another*, 87.

His family members, who want what's best for him but are held captive by the narratives of health care, visit him in the hospital. Berry describes what, in the context of a hospital, has become of his body:

> When they returned on yet another visit and found the old body still as it had been, a mere passive addition to the complicated machines that kept it minimally alive, they saw finally that in their attempt to help they had not helped but only complicated his disease beyond their power to help. And they thought with regret of the time when the thing that had been wrong with him had been simply unknown, and there had been only it and him and him and them in the place they had known together. Loving him, wanting to help him, they had given him over to "the best of modern medical care"—which meant, as they now saw, that they had abandoned him.[10]

The family of Burley Coulter had sought to abide with him, but instead they found they had done the opposite, they had abandoned him. Instead of being remembered, he had been dismembered by the "health care" system—known not in the context of his place, where memory properly resides, but known instead through knowledge of pathology through which the doctors knew him. For the doctors, Burley was a man whose body was diseased. For the people of Port William, Burley's body, sick as it was, was also the body of a father, a hunter, a farmer, a member. They knew his body's history, as well as some of the history that had preceded his body and the history of his offspring that would follow his body. This is the kind of knowledge that is whole and brings wholeness—health.

There was a time when medicine had access to this kind of knowledge, and there are still good doctors, who make use of it (though many will tell you that it is against the grain of their profession). But these doctors are increasingly disappearing, replaced by specialists and hospitalists. Get really sick and you will not see the doctor whose office one visits regularly, rather you will see a doctor who only works in a hospital. The doctor who knows your body

10. Berry, *Distant*, 376.

in a series of contexts, will then only know you by your charts, the filtered knowledge of your time within the system.

Danny Branch, Burley Coulter's son, cannot stand the way that his father's body has become dismembered. And so Danny breaks Burley out of the hospital, in a way that recalls a prison, to return home where he can die.

Danny hides his father in a barn as he begins to dig a grave for his father, a place where his father can be buried and return to the nutrient cycle of humus to humus, again working against state powers that ensure dismemberment.

It is in the barn that a kind of resurrection happens and Burley is restored to his body:

> Burley returned to his mind, and he knew him again as he had been when his life was full. He saw again the stance and demeanor of the man, the amused eyes, the lips pressed together while speech waited upon thought, an almost inviolable patience in the set of his shoulders. It was as though Burley stood in full view nearby, at ease and well at home—as though Danny could see him, but only on condition that he not look.[11]

Such resurrection could not happen without the remembering that must be placed. There in the barn where Burley and Danny had been together so often, it was not hard to see Burley without looking. His body was a presence in the place that had left its trace there—the place would never again be as though Burley had never existed.

This is starkly different from the reality if Burley had died in the hospital. There, he had no memory, because there was no trace of his life. Danny could not have "seen" him there—he could only have looked at his failing body, dismembered and made alien without so much as his father's own clothes.

11. Ibid., 408.

The Working Body

Burley was able to be re-membered because he had lived a bodily life, at home, in a place. He had worked there, grown food there, improved the place—his health was a result of his membership. But for many people in modern life we live without bodily membership in a place. Our health is instead guided and controlled by the health care system that is becoming an ever more pervasive presence. Our health becomes taking the supplements Doctor Oz tells us to take; it becomes exercising according the NIH recommendations. The increase of these health-system discourses has been concurrent with an ever sicker population—metabolically deranged, obese, diabetic.

Erwan Le Corre, a natural movement fitness teacher, describes modern human life as "life in the zoo." The zoo is where animals are taken out of their natural environments, given food in unnatural ways (i.e., without hunting), and the result is a regime of constant management by zookeepers to just keep the animals at the minimum of what would be easily maintained in their natural environments. Often, because they are unable to live natural lives, zoo animals become depressed and won't fulfill basic natural functions such as breeding. It is a sad existence and one that is not unlike modern life for human beings. Perhaps we could look at much of the health system as simply zoo keeping.

Steve Paxton, an important innovator in modern dance, said that his work has been an effort to "keep the search [for natural movement] alive in a culture which has engineered an environment which requires physical and sensorial suppression to exist in." Paxton goes on to say that in a city, "there is more neon than nuance and food is advertised rather than hunted for . . . It is appalling how we misuse the body; dance reminds us about that."[12] Physical work reminds us of that as well. I remember one day building garden rows with a friend who works a nine-to-five job in an office. As we worked our shovels into the ground, again and again, turning the soil it didn't take long for him to feel the work in his back and hands. But instead of complaining he said, "It feels good to actually work with my body." Most of us have had some experience of this—it is

12. Paxton.

rewarding to work with the body because it is *good* to work with the body. Such work gets at something essential about who we are—we were not made to spend our lives working only with screens and words and numbers. Our bodies are called to move.

Agrarianism helps us escape the zoo and get back to the work of the body and hands, delivering food that is whole and simple—kale, lamb, onions; no lessons in Greek and Latin pronunciation needed.

The abuse of the land is concurrent with the abuse of the body. To grow the corn and soybeans that are the building blocks of the foods that are fueling our health crisis, farmers sit long hours driving combines over land that is increasingly compacted and eroded and poisoned. Rather than being healthy through their work, farmers are as subject as anyone to obesity, their own bodies and the body of their land misused together.

Farmers like Elliot Coleman, a pioneering sustainable vegetable producer, work with and advocate the use of hand tools. These tools require the engagement of the body and just as importantly they allow for careful work on a landscape—work that results in the health of the land. The difference between a hand tool and a combine is the difference between carving wood with a chisel and a chainsaw, the wood can be carved with both, but at nowhere near the same level of care and artistry.

Coleman is well known for introducing traditional hand tools to American farmers and also for inventing and perfecting a few of his own to fulfill the particular tasks required of his land. Coleman represents a common aspect of many who work with hand tools—an honor for the tool itself. Those who work with their bodies honor the extensions of their bodies in their tools.

I have never felt any love for a power tool, but I have loved a hoe and a hammer. I suppose that I have loved a laptop (long since crashed and obsolete), but more so I have loved a pen I've had since high school and will, God willing, pass to my grandchildren—a possibility no laptop can enjoy. Wendell Berry writes of the beauty of a good tool in his essay, "The Good Scythe," where he compares his experience with a power scythe (a precursor to the weedeater) and a traditional European long-handled scythe.

The greatest difference between the good and bad scythe, Berry finds, was not in their ability to get the work of cutting grass and weeds done, but rather in how the two tools relate to the body. The good scythe is the one that works as an extension of the body, under the body's control and power. The bad scythe works apart from the body, subjecting the body to its pace and speed. As Berry writes:

> Using the hand scythe causes the simple bodily weariness that comes with exertion. This is a kind of weariness that, when not extreme, can be one of the pleasures of work. The power scythe, on the other hand, adds to that weariness of exertion the unpleasant weariness of strain. This is partly because, in addition to carrying and handling it, your attention is necessarily clenched to it—if you are to use it effectively and safely, you must not look away. Also it is partly because the power scythe, like all motor-driven tools, imposes patterns of endurance that are alien to the body. As long as the motor is running, there is pressure to keep going. You don't stop to rest or look around. You keep on until the motor stops or the job is finished or you have some kind of trouble.[13]

The difference here is the source of power. The traditional scythe works through the power of the body—it runs on breakfast. The power scythe or weedeater, however, works through a form of power that is alien to the body. The body becomes subject to a power external to itself and eventually the body is reduced to the level of the machine—a guiding apparatus to direct the power of the tool. To weedeat requires little skill or knowledge. To operate a scythe however requires both cognitive and physical intelligence; just watch a few videos of someone operating a scythe and it will be clear that working with a traditional scythe is a highly skilled act.

Ivan Illich has offered some of the most profound analyses of the ways in which technology relates to the body. Illich is particularly interested in the way in which tools became transformed from extensions of the hands to systems apart from the body. As Illich says in an interview with David Cayley:

13. Berry, *Gift*, 174–75.

> The computer . . . is not an instrument. It lacks a funda-
> mental characteristic of that which was discovered as an
> instrument in the twelfth century, the distality between
> the user and the tool. A hammer I can take or leave. It
> doesn't make me into part of the hammer. The hammer
> remains an instrument of the person, not the system. In
> a system the user, the manager, logically, by the logic of
> the system, becomes a part of the system.[14]

The history of technology has been one of deepening these sorts of systems. To go back to Berry's example, a scythe is clearly a tool—it is an extension of his person which he can pick up or not. The weedeater, or power scythe, however requires that Berry become a part of its system—it imposes its own patterns of work which are apart from the simple continuation of the system itself.

Another example might be the ways in which phones have been transformed from devices with which to make calls in to complete personal systems. We become iPhone users, more than iPhone owners. To purchase and use one we essentially lease them from the company, not really owning the phone without a stiff price. Our contract ensures that we become a part of the system, but then after two years are up we find that the phone has become a cybernetic extension. The dream of microchips in the brain will really be an innovation of convenience rather than a completely new system we must adopt.

A similar transformation is happening with the book. The shift from a physical paper book to an ebook is not simply a shift of medium, but rather a shift from a tool to a system. When a book becomes a Kindle text or iPad text, it becomes a part of a system that transforms the reading experience from a physical reality to something entirely different. The book is likely to change now that it is a part of this system—the book will disolve, if left to this form alone, into the web. Paper books are a stay against this disappearance, something like the keeping of traditional forms of tomatoes are a stay against the complete disappearance of quality tomatoes in the genetic homogeneity of the industrial system.

---

14. Cayley, *Rivers*, 204.

What is wonderful about a good book is the history of its reading. An old book in good condition is a collectible—an old book with marginalia and wine stains from a famous author is even more remarkable. There is a wonderful TEDTalk by the book designer Chip Kidd exploring some of these themes. After explaining the iconic covers he's created for books as varied as *Jurassic Park* and *1Q84*, Kidd goes on to explain why an ebook can never replace the physical book:

> Much is to be gained by eBooks: ease, convenience, portability. But something is definitely lost: tradition, a sensual experience, the comfort of thingy-ness—a little bit of humanity. Do you know what John Updike used to do the first thing when he would get a copy of one of his new books from Alfred A. Knopf? He'd smell it. Then he'd run his hand over the rag paper, and the pungent ink and the deckled edges of the pages. All those years, all those books, he never got tired of it. Now, I am all for the iPad, but trust me—smelling it will get you nowhere.[15]

This is as good a defense of the Incarnation as I know. Thingy-ness is where human beings dwell—and things are particulars, inescapably disappointments to the universal. Plato would have loved the web, in a way. It is a world of ideals, but it is not a world of bodies, it is not a place of reality—there is no shit on the Internet, there is no smell, no touch, no taste, no presence. All of this might make it an attractive place for some—it is after all a place where desires can run free from the bounds of real risks, death, and disease. When those desires escape from cyberspace to incarnational space, it is often recorded as a tragic and violent news story. Better, the agrarians would remind us, to have our desires formed in the plane of causations—my neglect will mean death, my carelessness crop loss, my care the possibility of flourishing.

15. Kidd, "Designing."

Word Made Flesh

With the disappearance of the body from work, we have completed a path that has long been at work in Western culture—the Gnostic temptation to see the things and work of the body as bad and the work of the mind as good. The ultimate of our economy is to be "knowledge workers"—how truly Gnostic this dream is! The Gnostic temptation has been a haunting challenge for the church from the beginning, because it is the temptation we are most drawn to—we are people of the spirit, not the flesh. It is critical for the church to remain faithful to the Christ who lived as a person with skin that could be pierced, bones that could be broken, blood that could be shed. We must remember that the word became flesh, not the other way around.

To serve a God who bleeds we must pay attention to the physical nature of our worship. The scriptures are filled with nauseatingly detailed accounts of the physical nature of worship, such as the Levitical laws on how to boil goat's meat or the many early Christian debates about eating meat sacrificed to idols. These details reflect the embodied nature of our faith—that this is a religion for people with bodies that matter and that is what makes Christian faith worthwhile. As Stanley Hauerwas has famously said, "Any religion that is worthwhile will tell you what to do with your pots and pans, and your genitals."

If we are searching for salvation, then it must be salvation of the body if it is going to be the salvation of people. What value is a religion that saves our souls and not our bodies? How can we save our bodies without saving the context, the ecosystems, on which they are dependent? A salvation of the soul without the body would leave us like Rumplestilskins—split down the middle of our selves.

Harold Bloom, the famous literary critic has said that Gnosticism is the "American religion"—a religion of individual divinity. We live lopsided. Agrarianism helps to free us of this imbalance and returns us to whole selves with complete bodies. In doing so it reminds us that individual divinity just won't do. When the separation of body from soul is undone we must face the reality of our bodies as connected—tied to the earth through the cycles of nourishment, of food and manure, of birth and death. Christ gave us bread and wine with which to remember him and participate in his life and death. Perhaps he also gave it to us so that we would be reminded that God ate and drank.

Some religions may believe the spiritually pure are completely freed of the need for food, but no Christian could believe such a thing. It is in food and drink that we find the God we worship, it is in eating his flesh and drinking his blood that we participate in his life. But in our practiced way of etherealizing the most physical—it is easy to make even the Eucharist a mere symbol—taking from it its power. Agrarianism reminds us, however, that the bread came from soil, that the wine came from grapes and microorganisms metabolizing its sugars. If we spend any time on a wheat farm or grape vineyard we may even find that manure is used as fertilizer, that the soil is built through death and decay. When you go to the communion rail, when you sit with that little cup and cracker, think on these things—the Body of Christ, the Bread of Heaven, the Blood of Christ, the Cup of Salvation—these have a history, a history that reaches back to the Last Supper, and into the geologic time of glacial deposits, the countless deaths and resurrections of generations.

5

No Small World

"The moment one gives close attention to anything,
even a blade of grass, it becomes a mysterious, awesome,
indescribably magnificent world in itself."
—HENRY MILLER

My grandfather often tells a story from his boyhood in rural Arkansas of a school trip to the county seat. The trip was only about twenty miles by bus, but this was before the widespread use of cars, and twenty miles was quite a distance—much farther than many of his classmates had ever traveled. Laughing, my grandfather tells of one boy who was particularly excited by the trip. Upon reaching the town this boy stepped off the bus, threw his arms above his head, and exclaimed: "Who would have known the world was so big!"

This is a funny story because the boy in it seems so backward, but it would be a mistake to miss the wisdom of his excitement. For this boy twenty miles had doubled his world, but this world was not the world of the modern urbanite. It was a world of deep intimacy, of connection, of knowledge. This boy knew most of the people in his community, as my grandfather did; he knew all of the good hunting, fishing, and trapping places, even the exact places where coons had been treed or big fish caught. It was a world that was vast in its own way, with more than enough space and change for an entire life to be played out. A twenty-mile trip had shown this boy only that there were places upon places where such lives could be lived, with other people who knew where the largest fish had been caught or the biggest buck killed. That a twenty-mile trip could take one to another such vast area could begin the imagination moving on to the next twenty miles and the next—each place with its own particular vastness. Who would have known the world was so big!

Compare this story with a conversation I once had at a dinner party. I talked with a woman who couldn't be more different from the boy of my grandfather's story. She was an elite of the new global economy—with no home but the world. This woman was an art historian and her husband was in finance. The two of them had met on a trip to Los Angeles while she was living in London and he in Paris. They carried on their courtship traveling to one another's cities and once married moved to Chicago, but planned to soon move to Beijing.

After talking for a while she got around to repeating one of the most tired mantras of the global economy, "Well, it is a small world after all." I would not deny that *her world* was small. She could just as well live in France as in England, the U.S. as in China. Her day to day life would change little from place to place. I have done my own bit of surface travel and though each place has its local differences, enough to keep it interesting, most international cities seem similar enough on the surface to be familiar even if one hasn't been there before. There are generally the same sorts of people in each city, doing the same sorts of business, with the same sorts of shopping, even the exact same restaurants. One can go to Starbucks in London, order a caramel macchiato, and forget that it isn't in Chicago except for the coins one gets in change. But to imagine that this façade of consumption is somehow the reality of a place is to miss something fundamental. Feeling that the world is small doesn't mean it is.

Each place from rural Arkansas to urban London has immense variation, and that variation goes deep and has a history. Someone who knows a place knows what that London Starbucks was before it was a Starbucks and what it was before that.

A quick urban trip will leave one with only the sense of passing landmarks. But to really see the difference of a place one must usually go to the edges—to the working class neighborhoods, to the outlying rural places. To know a place takes time, requires community, and forces one to listen. For this woman, it would take only ten minutes to find out where the nearest shopping district was. She just had to consult a guidebook or ask a passing person. For the boy on the bus it would have taken years to find out where the best deer woods were. It is not a question that one can just ask right away in a rural place. It requires time spent, connections made, acceptance. It is the sort of knowledge that is given, not bought, and is more tacit than spoken.

Novelist and critic John Berger compares this difference between the urban and the rural by way of the visceral. By "urban" Berger means the site of the international economy, the home of the transient classes. Berger writes that, "The ideal urban surface is a brilliant one which reflects what is in front of it, and seems to deny that there is anything visible behind it . . . The outside, the exterior, is celebrated by continuous visual reproduction (duplication) and justified by empiricism."[1] This urban surface is opposed to the rural or "peasant" reality of the visceral, the knowledge of what lies behind the surface. Berger says that for "the peasant the empirical is naïve . . . What is visible is usually a sign for him of the state of the invisible."[2]

This difference between the urban "exterior" and the rural "visceral" reality can be best seen through meat. For most urban people, and now unfortunately most rural people as well, meat is something that we have become abstracted from. We know in our heads that this meat was once a part of an animal. But for the most part we don't know exactly which part, nor do we really care to know. Most urban customers are satisfied to find their meat plastic wrapped in the grocery store—they want no part of the reality behind it, or increasingly they want no part of meat at all.

1. Berger, *Selected*, 520.
2. Ibid.

On the other hand a traditional rural person, a peasant, knows both the outside and inside of the meat on his or her table. Peasants know the life that the animal had before it reached their plate. As Berger has said elsewhere, "A peasant becomes fond of his pig and is glad to salt away its pork. What is significant, and is so difficult for the urban stranger to understand, is that the two statements in that sentence are connected by an *and* and not by a *but*."[3] The peasant knows what he is eating and is glad to have known it.

The difference between the small world and the large, the urban and rural, the visceral and exterior might be interesting for academics and intellectuals. But what is really the problem with a person not caring to know the sort of life an animal had before she eats its steak? What is the problem with living only in the world of the international city and not going to its borders to realize the deep differences between places? What is the problem with living in a small world rather than a large one?

The problem is a matter of care and its nature. To care we cannot act abstractly—care is always concrete. We might try to act responsibly toward people that we do not know, but true care, which is something more than responsibility, requires knowledge, experience, touch. If we do not really know a place then we will not care for it or know how to care for it.

Knowledge and ignorance are not opposites, but grow together. When one has knowledge of a place one realizes how little one knows about it. The proper response to this is care—watching where one steps, taking time to act. When we see only the surface we think that we know the reality of a place, but our ignorance does not grow with our knowledge. Here we are missing the truth of things.

As Bonhoeffer once said, "No good at all can come from acting before the world and one's self as though we knew the truth, when in reality we do not."[4] But to say that the world is small is to say that one knows it or can know it, and therefore can manage

3. Quoted in Watson, *The Whole Hog*, 91.
4. Bonhoeffer, *No Rusty Swords*, 159.

it. This is the "knowledge" of the expert—a sort of knowledge that does not grow with ignorance, but ignores it.

An example of this comes from an episode of the NPR program *This American Life*.[5] The program was on recycling, trash, and what the "truth" was about both. On the show they interviewed many experts in waste management and recycling and tried to find out if recycling really made a difference or not.

One expert on the show answered this last question by saying that recycling aluminum cans or paper did make a difference because for both of these less energy was required to recycle them than to make new products out of raw materials. But recycling glass, he went on to say, was a waste of time and resources because it takes the same amount of energy to recycle glass as to make new glass from raw materials. Sand, the raw material for glass, is not rare after all.

Such thinking is typical of experts who live in the abstract world of "energy." But such abstraction misses a very basic point that would make recycling glass important. That point is that the sand for glass must be mined, and it must be mined some place, and that some place has a certain ecosystem that will be disrupted by mining. The expert is living in the economy of finite measure, in this case energy, which to go back to Berry's "Two Economies" is woefully incomplete. If we are living in the kingdom of God we are brought again into an economy that cares for everything small and large.

I once lived near a sand mine that could have supplied a glass factory, and I watched over the years as it eroded a very valuable sand bar ecosystem along the Arkansas River. I know this because I lived there for years and I spent a great deal of time watching wildlife on that sand bar before the mine ever arrived. I have *witnessed* the difference.

We are left then with a choice. Are we going to live in a small world or a large one? The choice is one of great consequence and harbors harsh penalties. Whatever we choose, there can be no doubt what our age has chosen. The modern, industrial age lives in the

---

5. *This American Life* episode 249, aired October 31, 2003.

small world. It has sought to comprehend and subsume everything, to connect everything, and it has ignored what it cannot comprehend or connect. And what it has ignored it has often destroyed.

On the Road to the Small World

In the beginning of *The Unsettling of America*, Wendell Berry notes that "One of the peculiarities of the white race's presence in America is how little intention has been applied to it."[6] The joke goes that this continent was "discovered by an Italian who was on his way to India." That is to say that America was a land that was never really settled for itself—it was always a place on the way to something else. Gold, spices, trade routes—America was the first place to be formed by the new international economy that began, not with the WTO, but the Renaissance.

There were of course others who came before and after the conquistadors and explorers. There were people who came to stay put. But they have been the minority and often the victims of the more dominant trend toward movement.

Almost as quickly as America became settled it began to move, first through westward expansion, then through the coming of the Industrial Revolution and the shift of the economy from the farm to the factory. This history we all know from high school.

What is more interesting is what has happened after all of this, when the industrial economy became well established and spread nearly everywhere, when moving to find work became less necessary. Just when the possibility to settle seemed open is exactly the time when Americans began to move more than ever. Here we begin to understand that economic explanations of American transience are not sufficient. Americans move not because they must, but because of something deep in their character.

Perhaps our best guide to this character is Jack Kerouac's *On the Road*. So often taken to be a celebration of transience, I think *On the Road* is a painfully self-conscious exploration of the worst parts of American restlessness.

6. Berry, *Unsettling*, 3.

The novel is a thinly fictional account of a series of cross-country trips that Kerouac took with Neal Cassady. The two of them are in a search for Cassady's homeless father who's living on some street, somewhere. For both of them the trip is a search for some kind of home: for Cassady the lost home of his father, for Kerouac the home he lost through his broken marriage.

But neither one of them can really do the things they need to do to settle. They are compelled to keep moving by a desire to see everything and do everything. As Kerouac says early in the book, "I shambled . . . after people who interest me, because the only people for me are the mad ones, the ones who are mad to live, mad to talk, mad to be saved, desirous of everything at the same time."[7] This is the American sort of exuberance that comes when we are told "You're free to pursue happiness," but not what happiness is. Somehow along the way we began to feel that it is desire rather than satisfaction that gives us happiness. We want, like Kerouac, to "burn, burn, burn like fabulous yellow roman candles," not to settle down by the hearth.[8]

This replacement of desire for satisfaction has its roots, again, in the philosophy of John Locke, who gave us our understanding of property. Locke believed that "everything that God gives us is almost worthless except for our freedom."[9] As we've noted, this means that creation is left to us by God as a sort of raw material to be made valuable through our own labor and choices. We are free to do with it what we will—God is not still present to give it meaning or value. As Peter Augustine Lawler points out, this leaves us "free to pursue happiness, but never actually to become happy."[10] Since creation has no received meaning or value, the value given to it through our free action is as individual and fickle as the free person. Once we have obtained some desired result in the raw materials of nature we are left unsatisfied and begin to think of other ways we want to make

---

7. Kerouac, *On the Road*, 5.

8. Ibid.

9. Lawler, *Mars Hill Audio Journal*.

10. Ibid.

meaning. As Lawler says, the Lockeian person is "always thinking about what he doesn't have but might acquire through [his] work."[11]

Lawler opposes this Lockeian idea of freedom and happiness to Pascal's Christian vision of happiness. For Pascal our restlessness is what comes when we do not accept God as the giver of our lives. We constantly move from one desire to another because we are afraid of the emptiness that will show itself when we stand still with what we know. To go back to *On the Road*, at one point Kerouac describes a moment at a party in Colorado that points to such a feeling: "We were on the roof of America and all we could do was yell, I guess—across the night, eastward over the Plains, where somewhere an old man with white hair was probably walking toward us with the Word, and would arrive at any minute and make us silent."[12] Kerouac recognized that for all of his burning and restlessness that he would not find what he was looking for on the road, yet he couldn't find an exit.

Propelled on from place to place by the Lockeian restlessness of "happiness elsewhere," Kerouac becomes lost. He describes the realization of this as he woke up in a hotel on his way to Denver:

> I woke up as the sun was reddening; and that was the one distinct time in my life, the strangest moment of all, when I didn't know who I was—I was far away from home, haunted and tired with travel, in a cheap motel room I'd never seen, hearing the hiss of steam outside, and the creak of the old wood of the hotel, and footsteps upstairs, and all the sad sounds, and I looked at the cracked high ceiling and really didn't know who I was for about fifteen strange seconds. I wasn't scared; I was just somebody else, some stranger, and my whole life was a haunted life, the life of a ghost.[13]

This ghostly aspect is a symptom of the Gnostic nature of transience. To live as a part of a place is to live an incarnate, embodied life, but to live without place, driven by desire is to live without

11. Ibid.

12. Kerouac, *On the Road*, 50.

13. Ibid, 14.

embodiment—you are never really present anywhere. This is lostness in its most basic sense; lostness is simply "being out of place."

The problem with being out of place is that it makes it difficult to see the differences between things. I once lived in a small rural town where there was a convenience store that served breakfast and every morning ten or so farmers and loggers gathered to eat with each other and talk before work. They watched those coming in and out of the place and they knew who lived in town and who didn't. They would recognize a stranger coming in.

But for Kerouac and Cassady, searching for Cassady's father, the differences between things become indistinguishable. They don't know the regulars from the strangers. When Kerouac goes looking for Old Dean Moriarty (Cassady's father's name in the book) in the streets of Denver he couldn't see him even if he was there: "It seemed to me every bum on Larimer Street maybe was Dean Moriarty's father."[14]

It is not only the inability to see the differences between things that keeps Kerouac from finding what he's after. Ultimately it is that old problem that Augustine knew so well of taking a lesser good for a greater one. Kerouac knows that he really wants the greater good, as he tells Cassidy, "I want to marry a girl . . . so I can rest my soul with her till we both get old. This can't go on all the time—all this franticness and jumping around. We've got to go someplace, find something."[15] But it does go on and it goes on because Kerouac lets it go on.

This is the condition that so many of us in our consumer society find ourselves in. We know what we want, but always let smaller pleasures distract us from that deeper goal. The Slovenian philosopher Slavoj Zizek, following psychoanalyst Jacques Lacan, says that much of our modern, capitalist life is filled with the pursuit of an *object petit a*.[16] This is a technical term for the little pleasures of things that give us momentary happiness, but ultimately distract us from true pleasure.

14. Ibid., 52.
15. Ibid., 108.
16. Zizek, *The Fragile Absolute*, 11–39.

An example of this would be my own love for book shopping. I love to buy new books. I like looking through bookstores, feeling books in my hand, imagining all of the new possibilities of a novel or the new insights of a nonfiction book. I like the act of purchasing a book in itself. But while I am shopping for new books I am leaving scores of books that I already own unread. The true satisfaction of a book comes in reading it, but I often ignore that true satisfaction for the lesser satisfaction of buying a new book. Zizek says that modern consumer economies are built through the desire for these small pleasures that distract us from a truly satisfied life. Augustine would add to Zizek by saying that any pleasure other than one that rests in God is a small distracting pleasure.

Going back to Kerouac then we could say that Kerouac continually gets distracted by the small pleasure of restless travel and is prevented from ever actually finding the true, settled pleasure he desires. This, we could say, is the modern American condition.

This condition is always telling us that life will be better elsewhere, that a new job will satisfy us more, that a new church will be more to our liking. So we move and move and move again. This is how we begin to miss the depths of the world that take time to see, that require patience and settledness. Agrarianism offers us a way out of this unsettledness. The agricultural way of life forces us to stay put, to wait and see what might appear from beneath the soil.

Knowing One's Place

For Locke the world is like some bad birthday, full of gifts that we didn't ask for and don't need. To make it meaningful we have no choice but to exchange them and turn them into cash for something more to our liking. But for the agrarian tradition the world is a gift nothing short of miraculous. Creation is given by God and we ourselves are a part of the gift. It is not our role to give the world meaning and value—it already has these. Our part is to be what we were made for; our part is to flourish.

That the creation is a divine gift should give us hope, but it also means that we must live with caution. God is involved here, and with God and his things we must always be careful. Wendell Berry writes that the divine givenness of the world "places us in a position of extreme danger."[17] We are not just living among raw materials, we are living as a part of a created order Christ himself died to restore.

The only response to this danger can be the response of Christ, Berry writes. We must have a "love for everything that exists, including our enemies."[18] But how do we do this with creation?

To begin we must recognize the things of creation for what they are—unique creatures in unique places. As Berry writes, "to say that life is a miracle . . . is to insist upon the uniqueness and the value of individual creatures; it is to set creatures free from generalizations about them."[19]

As I write this I look out my window and I see my flock of laying hens. Each of these is a chicken, and beyond that every one of them is a unique combination of breeds. They have different markings and personalities. They are all individuals. It may seem strange to speak this way of an animal, but anyone who has had a pet knows this. The problem is that in the industrial mind we do not treat things as unique. We raise chickens. We teach children. We grow soybeans. Little attention is paid to the uniqueness of each one of these. If a chicken cannot handle being confined with a thousand other chickens in a chicken house, we don't change the system, we change the chicken by giving it antibiotics. If a child does not fit well with the industrial system of education we do not change the system, we prescribe Ritalin.

The animal husband, the good farmer, the good teacher will have none of this. Because they act from love they will respond to the unique creature in itself. As Berry relates, a horse trainer was once asked "How do you train horses?" to which he responded "Which one do you have in mind?"[20]

---

17. Berry, *Citizenship Papers*, 182.

18. Ibid.

19. Ibid., 184.

20. Ibid.

To know the uniqueness of things one must pay attention to them. This means that we have to spend time doing it. In his carousing book *The Supper of the Lamb*, the Episcopal priest Robert Farrar Capon recommends that we spend an hour peeling an onion for lamb stew. The purpose in this is to pay attention to the onion—to realize what it is in itself. For many this may seem like something for someone with too much time on their hands, but for Capon it is nothing less than the practice of humanity's real work. "Man's real work is to look at the things of the world and to love them for what they are," he writes. "That is, after all, what God does, and man was not made in God's image for nothing. The fruits of his attention can be seen in all the arts, crafts, and sciences."[21] Who would have thought to catch a wild forest bird and domesticate it so that it would become the most common dinner meat? Who looked at a log, animal skins, and animal tendons long enough to make the first drum? The world is built on paying attention. The work of paying attention is the only sort of work that can never be outsourced or done by a machine because paying attention means paying attention in a specific place to specific things. As Berry writes, "No machine could perform work resembling that of Paul Cezanne or any good farmer, because the work of both presupposes a specifically human life's devotion to the practice of an art and to love for a specific landscape."[22]

Such work with a specific landscape seems romantic in our age when few of us have had the experience of such work. The farmer and writer Gene Logsdon offers his neighbor as one who has accomplished it. "Dave Haferd sees his farm with eyes that are 200 years old," Logsdon writes. "He knows every foot of its 180 acres, on top and underneath. Walking across his land, he discourses endlessly and joyfully upon almost any rock, post, tree, clod, weed or building that his eye falls upon."[23] Dave Haferd knows his land by birth, tradition, and work. But he also knows it because he has paid attention while working and listened to what his elders told

21. Capon, *Supper of the Lamb*, 19.
22. Berry, *Citizenship*, 183–84.
23. Logsdon, *Living*, 100.

him about the place. Haferd tells Logsdon that they always keep red clover in rotation on the place, even if they don't make hay from it and just plow it under. "Oh yes, it still pays if you only plow it under," he says, "*This* ground would not last without a regular plow down of clover. And it's the greatest help in weed control. We learned that long ago."[24] The same might not go for another place, but Haferd has learned it for his. It is this specific knowledge that keeps a place going and growing food. If one does not pay such attention to the individual place one can damage it to infertility.

The central agrarian understanding of place is that we are to live "a given life in a given world." This means, as Berry points out, that "our ability to change either our life or our place is limited."[25] Like the other creatures of the earth we must learn to adapt to our places in our habits and our technology.

Our modern problem is that we have become too good at changing the place to fit to our desires. If we live in a hot place we don't have to build breezeways to make our summers bearable, we only have to turn on the air conditioner. But unlike a breezeway where we can see all of the costs and benefits, the air conditioner comes with hidden costs. It entails the mining of coal in Pennsylvania or the disposal of nuclear waste in Utah; it entails mercury pollution in lakes and rivers, and other costs still unknown. We pretend that we have solved the problem of summer heat without adaptation, when we have only created hidden problems.

This became particularly clear to me one day when I went to an EPA hearing on air pollution from coal burning power plants. It was a hot, humid summer day with temperatures approaching 100 degrees F. Most of the people sitting in the room were in suits and the air conditioner was running full blast to make the room comfortable. One of the first people to testify was a man from a community group. He was neatly dressed, but stood out because he was wearing shorts, and a short-sleeved shirt. When he got to the podium the first thing he said was, "I think it's a little ironic that we are here discussing the damaging pollution of coal fired

24. Ibid., 104–5.
25. Berry, *Citizenship*, 184.

power plants when it is summer and everyone here is wearing dark, heavy suits so we have to run the air conditioner." The man was right. Most of the people in the room were not paying attention to the given weather and were using damaging resources to adjust the world to themselves rather than themselves to the given world. We know that such inattention can damage the world, but what about the soul?

Dallas Willard has written that, "The soul is that dimension of the person that interrelates all of the other dimensions so that they form one life. It is like a meta-dimension or higher-level dimension because its direct field of play consists of the other dimensions (thought, body, and so on), and through them it reaches ever deeper into the person's vast environment of God and his creation."[26] Each of our particular places might be best understood as our soul. Our "place" is that space in which all the aspects of our self are collected. This is to go much deeper than physical place, but physical place does play a role here. As we noted with Kerouac to be "out of place" is to be lost. We would not of course say that one who does not pay attention to his or her physical place is lost in the spiritual sense, but I do think that to see lostness as only spiritual is to miss something important. Physical transience has often reflected spiritual transience, both in reality and as a metaphor.

I think that so much of our modern emphasis on "personal" and "individual" salvation apart from the community of the church comes because we are physically lost. We do not know how to think of the place of the local church in salvation when we live the rest of our life floating without locality or substantial community. If we are to pay proper attention to our soul, then we must take seriously the context in which we live, our "vast environment of God and his creation."

Healing

Wendell Berry once put a pond on a hillside of his farm where he hoped to make a pasture. He consulted the experts, he studied the

26. Willard, *Renovation*, 37.

books, but the pond did not hold. It broke and left a scar on his land. It was not a large pond and with time the land will heal itself. But as Berry writes, "there *is* damage—to my place, and to me. I have carried it out, before my own eyes and against my intention, a part of the modern tragedy."[27] We have all done this in some way; we have damaged our land because we have not paid attention to it. We have thought that we understood our place, but we have not let our knowledge grow with our ignorance. Our place has been damaged and so we too have been damaged.

Healing can come only through careful and creative work. This good work Berry writes, "finds the way between pride and despair . . . It preserves the given so that it remains a gift."[28] We cannot create the possibility of this healing; we only participate in it as creatures. To have this health is "to keep oneself fully alive in the Creation, to keep the Creation fully alive in oneself, to see the Creation anew, to welcome one's part in it anew."[29] It is a gift we must be home to receive.

27. Berry, *People*, 6.
28. Ibid., 10.
29. Ibid., 9.

6

Dirt Time

"Clocks slay time ... time is dead as long as it is being clicked off by little wheels; only when the clock stops does time come to life."
—WILLIAM FAULKNER, *The Sound and the Fury*

One summer solstice, while I was an apprentice farmer, I went with my mentor to deliver a load of sheep to an Amish farm in the Arkansas River valley. It was late in the day, the sun spreading long shadows across the pasture, and we hurried the sheep off the trailer to get them settled before dark. "They say it's the longest day of the year, but I still don't have enough time," my mentor remarked as we herded the sheep into a pen. "Oh, there's always enough time," the Amish farmer replied with a smile.

If agrarianism can help reorient our understanding of space, and call us to an economy of abundance, then it must also change our understanding of time. As with everything else, "there is always enough" is the basic statement of the agrarian economy of time. And again, this stance of abundance stands in stark contrast to the industrial society where "there is never enough time in the day." In the economy where "time is money," where we are "buying time" and "spending it," trying with all our might not to "waste it," time is a scarce commodity. Yet it is a strange commodity because it is of completely fixed supply. Unlike money it cannot be made or printed. It does not risk deflation or inflation—it simply is, there, however we relate to it. It is open to anyone and everyone equally and the poor are as likely to have it in quantity as the rich are—sometimes more so.

The difference between agrarian and industrial time lies on two levels. First there is the level of the daily rhythm of time, how the hours are marked off through the day, the way in which we relate to the raw hours of time with speed or slowness, with work or idleness. Second there is a different relationship to the telos of time, to the whole scope and purpose of time within which we are working. There is an overlap between the daily and the teleological levels, as we will see, but it will be helpful to explore each, and the practices that make them manifest, in turn.

Liturgy of the Hours

There are days that stretch out, where we are fully present in our work, in our conversations, in each activity—there is no rush. These times are slow. We are tempted to completely miss time; to let it pass by without the acknowledgment of a clock. Here time is simply a part of being—the fact of temporality. We may have things to do within this time, but our work is focused on the level of being—our interaction with a person, with a thing. This is agrarian time—time that reflects a balance of limits and focus, of doing the work that needs doing and not trying to do more than that.

Against this is industrial time, which is tied to an economy that must always produce more from a limited and scarce series of resources in order to continue its trajectory of growth. Here time is both limited and limitless—all time becomes productive, forced into a regimen of time management. This is the time where factories never sleep, where we can buy a toaster at 2 AM, where we can eat a "Fourth Meal" at a drive-through in the middle of the night. Sleep and rest are problems here because they have not yet been fully comodified—if only we could buy and sell in our dreams.

The pace of the industrial time is speed—always more speed. We are willing to sacrifice a great deal for this speed: the great number of lives lost through high-velocity car accidents go relatively unquestioned. But more than this we sacrifice a good deal of our health through expedience, through the tired nights we give over to getting more done.

Speed is always on the side of violence, whether it is the breeding of a chicken for rapid growth or in a coup d'état. Slowness is the companion of consensus, of listening, of waiting for all voices to be heard—it is the pace of the human, who is after all, Imago Dei. Our slowness, violated in the industrial, mechanized world, is nothing but the slowness of God; a God who is willing to wait on a cross in order to accomplish the work of love. We are lost if we do not slow down to the pace of that love.

Kosuko Koyama, writing to the church in Singapore, a completely urbanized nation that has adopted speed perhaps even more than the United States, asks:

> Is not the biblical God an "inefficient" and "slow" God because he is the God of the covenant relationship motivated by love? The image of the crucified Christ ("nailed down"—the ultimate symbol of immobility, the "maximum slowness") is an intensification of the forty years wandering in the wilderness.[1]

We have lost our slowness, our sense of the wandering, "nailed down" God in part because we have been "uprooted 'from the ground,'" Koyama writes. "Distance from the ground is causing psychological problems. 'To be human' is to be 'on the gound' . . . Theological 'erets-ology' is needed (erets = earth in Hebrew, see Gen. 1:1)."[2] Agrarianism, as we have argued, provided exactly this erets-ology, bringing theology back to the necessary slowness of the human by reminding us of the soil from which we live.

The soil and a life lived in response to it creates a kind of liturgy of the hours—a way of moving the work of human community into holy time. When we respond to the soil and *abad* it (serve it, as we

1. Koyama, *Water Buffalo*, 4.
2. Ibid.

are called to do in Genesis 2:15) we are welcomed into a rhythm of life that both directs our attention, but also moves our bodies into a time to which it can keep pace—in this way our work becomes a kind of dance. Breathing and eating, birth and decay—these guide the rhythms of the agrarian hours. The morning is for watering plants because watering in the evening could create root diseases. Animals eat at certain times and are expectant of a regular pattern of feedings. Seasons come and go, changing the dance's tempo—the afternoons become too hot in the summer or the mornings too cold in the winter. On a hot day, when the temperatures reach past 100 and all animals are quiet except the cicadas who have been waiting twenty years to sing, it is only humans who keep working. We do so at great expense, requiring a great output of energy, mostly fossil fuels to putter around in our air-conditioned tractor cabs. The natural pattern of life is one of work and leisure, a call and response of effort and idleness. But we have lost the liturgy of soil and seasons and accepted the limitless appetite for growth of an idol "economy" that demands in a perverse liturgy, like the Mayan gods of Tikal, a daily sacrifice of human blood just to make the sun rise. The human is subsumed into the rhythms of the machine. To break free from this perverse liturgy of the machine and reclaim the liturgy of the soil we can begin the work by claiming a place and a practice.

A Place of Agrarian Time: The Porch

One of the great symbols of agrarian society has been the rocking chair and the front porch, both now reduced to Cracker Barrel nostalgia. In the mid-1800s, when he was attempting to articulate the difference between American and English space, the landscape designer Andrew Jackson Downing held the front porch as the key American place. It is a symbol of a slower pace of life, but it is also a statement of openness and conviviality—the front porch is essentially democratic, the space where our private lives intersect with the public. But perhaps, as a mark of democracy's decline into electoral mob rule as we see in our contemporary politics, the front porch is a disappearing feature of American life. Suburban houses tend to lack front porches and even increasingly front doors. Garages have become the most prominent feature in the front of many houses, with doors either off the garage or hidden around a corner from the street.

The porch, like many aspects of agrarian culture, is essentially a practical place. It is on the porch that people sat in the days before air conditioning while the house cooled off in the evening. My mother talks about her days growing up in a Delta Arkansas town where everyone would gather on their porches and lawns in the evening to cool off. It was easy to get to know your neighbors at that time—they were not just a car disappearing into a garage.

Yet with the invention of the air conditioner—a thing most Southerners and an increasing number of northerners would count among necessities—the front porch began to fade away. The air conditioner—itself a toxic thing that relies on carcinogenic refrigerants and electricity—rendered obsolete the front porch as a cooling off place. The decline of American democracy might be said to lie at the feet of Carrier.

The porch, however, like so much else in agrarian culture, has an enduring goodness that is brought back again and again. I am happy to see new houses going up, eschewing the trends of the nineties, with long front porches. There are even cultural movements setting out to reestablish the wonders of the front porch. The Professional Porch Sitters Union is a kind of anarchic association that invites people anywhere to set up a Union Local on their own porch and get to sitting with their friends and neighbors.

"The Professional Porch Sitters Union is about not planning anything. Anybody can call a meeting at any time, and attendance is optional," the Professional Porch Sitters Union's founder, Claude Stephens said in an interview with NPR. This is the true spirit of the porch. Sit down and who knows what will happen. A neighbor might bring over a beer, another might stop just to chat about tomatoes while looking over a front yard garden, and someone else might bring an instrument to play.

The primary function of the porch, as we have said, is a place for democratic conversation. When we sit on our porches we open ourselves to whomever might come by and this opens us to the uncomfortable. My wife and I often sit on our porch and sometimes this means we are called on to help people who otherwise would simply pass by our house. We wave a hello and the next thing we know we're running a passerby to Walgreens or airing up a kid's bike tire. It also means we say hi to Ms. Vera as she weeds her garden or talk to the retired priest around the corner who walks by enjoying the weather.

These conversations are slow. They are a way of getting to know each other. They are what form the withness of community. Even the most homogeneous suburban neighborhood contains enough diversity to create uncomfortable conversations between neighbors, but as we move from our front porches into the domains of our private space we are increasingly insulated from such conversations. We go into our houses, watch the channels that tell the truth as we see it, read the websites that make us nod our heads, and increasingly through Internet filtering systems, we see only the results that match our interests. Facebook for instance will show us mostly the "friend feeds" of those it determines we want to see, which often means those who share our political leanings. On the street we don't choose who we interact with. We meet whoever comes by, but in our private space we control it all. What Facebook and the like do is privatize our social life. We begin to filter the conversations of our friends into only the tidbits and articles and memes that interest us—Facebook is no digital front porch.

To agree with others with whom we share a worldview—that is expedient and easy. It takes time and lots of conversation to work through issues with those whom we disagree. If we are in a hurry, rather than wait through conversation, we will use violence and coercion to establish our way. This violence might be the rule of 51 percent through a vote or it might be an all-out war—either way, it is expedient and fast compared to the work necessary for consensus—a long path toward common understanding.

It is only through a return to porch sitting or yard sitting—of placing ourselves in the liminal space between public and private—that we can open ourselves to the difficult conversations that might lead to radical democracy. It is time to dust off our rocking chairs and sit a spell.

When I was in high school I once volunteered as an election monitor. I was placed in a very small rural polling place in Birdtown, Arkansas. I was about sixty years younger than most of the other monitors, and I listened to all of their stories about the old times. They said that in the old days everyone in the community would come together for the election. There would be a picnic, sometimes political speeches, and most importantly a big barrel of moonshine free to all. It was in that atmosphere that the decisions of the community were made. I'm suspicious now of most elections, but this seems to be the right way to hold one. It seems like the kind of election that extends from the practice of porch sitting where everyone has time, and anyone who takes it all more seriously than the gospel is likely to get ribbed.

A Practice of Agrarian Time: Cooking

Speed and slowness in growing food is of course only a corollary of speed and slowness in eating. Fast food is the result of inhuman speed—it is the direct result of the automobile. Without cars and the interstates that drove them to be a ubiquitous feature of American life, there simply would be no "fast" food as such. There have always been foods of convenience. A hunk of ham and biscuit as a meal for a field worker, a tamale. But food designed to be produced quickly and eaten quickly, modeled on industrial efficiencies, came about in the age of the car—starting with drive-in restaurants and then driven forward by the innovations of Ray Kroc at McDonalds.

In answer to this fast food we have a movement for slow food—which is really just to say traditional food ways. Here we are called to enjoy food not as a convenience but as a source of conviviality (the Slow Food organizations call their local chapters "Convivia"). It is through slowing down, and taking the time and care to cook, that we begin to truly discover the fullness of God's abundance in creation.

If there is one evangelical practice for agrarianism, cooking would be it. Cooking is a required discipline of agrarianism and when it is learned, it empowers anyone to save money, take the reins of their means of production, and eat according to their conscience rather than the whimsy of a restaurant.

My first forays into cooking came when I was living in Chicago, fresh out of college. There was a small organic grocery store near my apartment that offered subscriptions to weekly produce boxes from local farmers. My apartment mate and I signed up and were then forced to eat a box full of produce a week. Many of the boxes' contents were a mystery to us: Kohlrabi, Bak Choi, Daikon Radish, Swiss Chard, even Kale were new to us. We would type each ingredient into Epicurious.com and find a recipe we could use to prepare it. Over time I began to understand the ins and outs of cooking and the recipes began to be starts for improvisation. I became pretty good at cooking and started inviting friends over to share our meals with us. Pretty soon one of our friends agreed to bring beer or wine every Thursday in exchange for a meal. We all learned that year the pleasures and conviviality of cooking, and I began to see that if I wanted to convince people of a different way of eating, the best way would be to invite them to dinner.

Cooking, it is often said, is another lost art of our age. The greatest reason for its demise, I think, is a false understanding of convenience. We think that cooking is too time-intensive and that eating out or eating processed foods is fast and convenient. This myth is perpetuated by the processed food companies who show struggling families happily eating home cooked meals through the miracle of Tyson Family "Just-Microwave-It" Meals. But in my experience cooking my own food takes less time than it takes to run down the road and pick up food from a drive-through window (and I live pretty close to some drive-through windows). It is more a mentality about food and cooking than the actual act that hangs us up.

Robert Farrar Capon, in his beautiful and funny book *The Supper of the Lamb*, introduces a key concept that has forever changed my view of cooking—ferial and festal cooking. Capon says that ferial cooking is everyday kind of cooking—good cooking that leaves no waste and stretches out a meal. This is the kind of cooking my grandmothers did, using what they had to create a meal. Festal cooking on the other hand is a steak with asparagus—it is cooking that is meant for celebration, but is not as easy on the budget. Unfortunately (and this is perpetuated by the Food Network) festal cooking has become what people think of when they think of cooking. Ferial cooking has fallen by the wayside and people are doomed to think that they have no alternative but to eat convenience food or "cook" a four-course meal like they saw on TV. But the recovery of ferial cooking is the way that home cooking must be restored both from the perspective of expense and time.

With ferial cooking our creativity is engaged. We stare into the refrigerator and imagine what we can make of the random assortments we find. We have a dozen eggs, onions, some cheese, and in the garden Swiss chard needs to be picked—this can become a delicious frittata. Eggs, sweet potatoes, and some kale can easily turn into sweet potatoe fries, a fried egg, and a side of kale. The temptation is to think that this kind of ferial cooking isn't convenient—I've had those tired days where a pizza sounds like the trick. But there has never been a time when I've rallied, made a ferial meal, and been disappointed

Cooking at home also has the advantage of allowing you to cook according to your best desires for food. If you want a meal made of local food using only meat from farms that you trust treated their animals with care, then you can have it. This is simply not the case with the vast majority of restaurants. Cooking at home, ferial cooking provides freedom.

When cooking at home is not an option, we must not immediately assume compromise. This is not to say that I always eat in pure holiness or that we always can eat according to our best desires, but one practice that I find helpful in disciplining my eating has been the practice of fasting. Fasting helps us change our relationship with food by teaching us that goodness tastes better than having to eat. Fasting is a way of saying, "we will wait for something better."

The End of Time

The abundance or scarcity of time comes down to the expanse of it—whether we are "getting ours while we can" or whether we are working as a part of an economy that only makes sense on the scale of millennia. It depends also on our orientation toward time's end, whether we are working primarily for a future present or an ancient future.

The industrial economy is oriented to the future present. Its motivation is the preservation of wealth in a world of shrinking resources. If one listens to the industrial agronomists they can hardly speak without mentioning the rapidly rising global population, the threat of global warming, and diminished water resources as part of the reason their work is necessary. As Wendell Berry has often remarked, industrial agriculture is sold as either essential for feeding the world or the inevitable result of a progress more powerful than any human agency. Scarce water, growing populations, global warming are real worries, but they are particularly troubling for an economy that is in large part responsible for them. The push for more productive agriculture, for education regimes, for industrialization and economic development are in many ways efforts to preserve the status quo. The industrial economy only knows "progress," it only knows growth, it only knows how to orient itself into a more developed and advanced present. It is unable to imagine a radically new and different possibility.

Because of its roots in modernism, which was always rooted in a break from tradition and the past, the industrial economy can only look back in disdain. Nostalgia takes the form of a commodity, but when anyone begins to recommend some real turn back, such as the end of automobiles rather than simply greening the current modes of transportation, the move is too radical. We may like to have nice pens and typewriters, but most people would rather not return to them, even if it would mean a more just and sustainable world. Thus the response of anger when Wendell Berry suggested he wouldn't buy a computer. The past is past in the industrial world and the future is something we will always achieve through our ingenuity.

The agrarian economy on the other hand has an ancient-future orientation. It is a way of relating to time that recognizes the formation of reality by those who preceded and also looks toward the continued cultivation of reality into the future of the landscape.

The agrarian mind understands the role of human agency. It does not bow to the inevitability of "progress" but rather questions the past, seeking its wisdom, but also critical of its mistakes. It would be foolish not to build upon and work within the landscape created by earlier generations, but sometimes this will certainly mean undoing past damage. Yet even the undoing of damage offers us a lesson about the place—we know that hillside is no place for a pond, but these are lessons that we are likely to forget if we have no stability in the transfer of wisdom about a place. We can only build such stability by staying and being teachable.

I once visited a Cistercian monastery that was being newly built to the standard of two thousand years. They expected to be around a long time and they were building their monastery in the hills of East Oklahoma with that expectation. In contrast the suburban housing developments that are sprawling from cities in every direction are built to the standard of the quick buck—cheap housing for families that will not occupy those places in a decade much less a millennia. There is no expectation of staying, of building a lifescape for generations to come, and so the speed of their construction sets them up for the speed of their demise. The wasteland of Detroit is no accident—it is the natural result of a city built around the production of speed.

Agrarian time is slow because it has been disciplined by the soil that takes time. When we nurture the abundance of the soil we are welcoming the work of millennia—harvesting what we did not plant and planting what we will not harvest. To truly understand the source of the life we nurture we must recognize that the real work has come before us, often long before us, and that the true results of our own work, for good or ill, will last far into the future. What is an expedience now will be damage later. What is a slow cultivation now will be a fecund abundance in the future.

This orientation offers an important corrective to the church. Too many churches mimic and baptize the industrial orientation to the future. The focus becomes the production of an ever more relevant church with an increasing influence in the culture while at the same time expecting that that future will end in some momentous Rapture. Certain strains of Protestant evangelicals represent this to the extreme—history plays very little role, with the New Testament floating as an island without context. What is necessary now is the conquest of people, of culture, of politics using all of the tools of industrialism. It is no wonder that such churches actively rely on knowledge from sales, marketing, and entertainment.

The agrarian view, the ancient-future view, seeks the cultivation of flourishing here, now, and in the future. It is oriented to the redemption of this place and the bodies dependent on this place. Here we move closer to historic Christianity's expectation of time, where we begin with a fall and have been working through the history of the world toward redemption. Our work is not oriented toward some heaven in the sky, but a redemption of the world that God so loved. This is work we do in the places we build through the communities we are a part of.

In the Christian view our lives are oriented toward being faithful to the call and gifts we have been given. We do not orient our lives around some future promise but rather on the faithful work we are called to here and now. This is why we do not go to war, even though war might accomplish the ends that we hope for, because our call is not toward progress but faithfulness. In the same way, the good farmer is not called to make her farm as productive as possible so that she might feed the world. She is called to be responsible toward its gifts—the clean stream that runs through it, the stand of hardwood timber on the back forty, the rich soil on a hillside terrace. She may be able to grow more food, more quickly, and make more money and feed more people, but she would have to do so by violating her faithful care for these gifts. In doing so she is honoring the history of her place, the history of herself, the history of the wisdom that enables her to care. Her work toward the future is the passing on of that history, which must always be reiterated in a new time. For the agrarian, and the Christian, history is a continuum. For the industrial mind it is a series of violent disruptions.

Sabbath

We would miss an important and critical aspect of agrarian time if we did not touch again on the Sabbath, and so I want to close this chapter with some thoughts on what is both a place and a practice. There is much that can be said about the Sabbath and I would recommend Norman Wirzba's *Living the Sabbath* for a more extensive agrarian reading, so here we close with a taste of what is a feast.

The Rabbi Abraham Joshua Heschel in his classic book *The Sabbath* calls the Sabbath day a "palace in time with a kingdom for all."[3] To name it as such makes the Sabbath into a place—yet a place that stands outside of the world of things. In this palace in time we are invited to step out of the world of clocks, out of time as a measured pace, and to enter into divine time, which exists without tense. The Sabbath is a time to delight and delight is something best experienced in the "fullness of time," in which we relax into a magnificent present that fully encompasses both past and future. In this palace we live in a magnitude of grace.

In order to enter this place we must also practice the Sabbath, which means that we must follow its etiquette and laws or else we will no longer be allowed in the palace. This means that we must give up our striving, our efforts for accomplishment. We must be willing to leave things undone and be willing to let profits and production go. We must be willing to stop exploiting the work of others—people, animals, land.

The palace in time of the Sabbath is a place where God is God and we can be his children. We are welcomed there with delight—with the overwhelming abundance of grace as manifest in creation. The Sabbath is then an essential agrarian place because it is here that we celebrate the abundance of creation. There is enough of everything.

The Sabbath is unavailable to an industrial world that insists on scarcity, that must continue to strive in order to hold on to a manufactured abundance. In rejecting the grace of time and creation, in insisting that progress and technology take the place of God—the world fulfills its worst nightmares and becomes a desert

3. Heschel, *Sabbath*, 21.

devoid of life. All of those fields that are the bread basket of the world are sick, they are overworked and kept alive only with money and mining. One day, they will be given their rest because the industrial economy will inevitably collapse.

The agrarian on the other hand will rest now, let God be God and accept the grace of the world. In this there is a future for people in a place, learning its past lessons, caring for its present gifts, building its future. Investing in the millennium, we will plant sequoias.

7

Humility: The Recovery of Fear

"We have put aside a light burden which is self-accusation
only to take up the heavy one which is self-justification."
—John the Dwarf

"In truth, O Lord, if we do not know how to humble
ourselves you will never cease to humble us."
—Isaac the Syrian

The call to reality, to live in the truth rather than the illusions of
technological desire, is a call to the soil—to the most basic reality of
what we are. The reverse is also true; the call to the soil is a call to
reality. This is why agrarianism is so critical in an age when our lives
have been systematically separated from the soil and separated,
through as many technologies as possible, from our very real dependence upon the soil's fate. Agrarianism helps to remind us not
only that soil should be among our highest level concerns, but also
tells us that so much of our care and knowledge are locked clearly
in the grip of hubris. To hubris, agrarianism offers humility—a way
of seeing and being that enables us, as Saint Bernard of Clairvaux
said, to "live in the truth."[1]

1. Bernard, *Humility*, 29.

Hubris, Wendell Berry writes in his essay "The Way of Ignorance," is "ungodly ignorance disguised as godly arrogance."[2] "We identify arrogant ignorance," writes Berry, "by its willingness to work on too big a scale, and thus to put too much at risk. It fails to foresee bad consequences not only because some of the consequences of all acts are inherently unforeseeable, but also because the arrogantly ignorant often are blinded by money invested: they cannot afford to foresee bad consequences."[3]

Our history, particularly modern, is littered with examples of such hubris—the engineering capacity to drill deep in the ocean, but not the genius to stop a leak when it happens; the ability to create aerosols, but not the ability to prevent them from ripping a hole in the ozone layer; the ability to create nitrogen fertilizers that increase crop yields, but not the ability to keep those fertilizers from polluting waterways.

We act with great power, but not with great knowledge—however impressed we might be with what we know. Even our best engineers and scientists, acting beyond their proper understanding, have technologies that are not unlike "a loaded pistol in the hands of a monkey," as Berry puts it.[4] We are enamored by the shiny things of our power, but we cannot even begin to understand their consequences.

Such ignorant arrogance is at the roots of human sin. It was hubris that began our falleness, what Dietrich von Hildebrand calls "Satanic pride." The one who possesses such pride, writes Hildebrand, "knows one kind of satisfaction only: the glorification of the self. For him, the entire world is devoid of interest except insofar as it offers him an opportunity to experience his own superiority, power, and splendor."[5] Does this not describe industrial society? We are deeply impressed at our technological prowess, our ability to control and create. And yet, to maintain our pride we must be "blind to value"; we must be "unable to grasp the inherent beauty and nobil-

2. Berry, *Ignorance*, 53.
3. Ibid., 54.
4. Ibid., 53.
5. Hildebrand, *Humility*, 9.

ity of objective values."[6] This Satanic pride, which Hildebrand also calls metaphysical pride, "fails to perceive the indissoluble union between all-powerfulness and all-goodness; he would separate omnipotence from all-goodness and attribute the former to himself."[7]

Blind to all external or objective value, we are drawn into a kind of solipsism of ourselves. Such temptations are easy in places where the surface becomes the reality, as Berger pointed out regarding cities. New York may begin to see its reality as necessary, critical even, just as Rome saw its reality as central. But such places do not exist without countrysides and it is through ignoring this fact that the flourishing of the countryside is not encouraged. With its ground mined rather than cultivated the countryside is colonized rather than celebrated.

The tenuous nature of our society hides behind our technology—but always there is the real possibility that it could all come to a crashing halt. As I write, in a heat wave and drought that is beyond anything on record, power failures have left large sections of the country without electricity. For now such outages are limited in geography and time, but they show us just how fragile our technologies are. With a disruption to the oil or electricity supply our society would come to a crashing halt. Yet we pretend that we are masters of the universe, impressed with our iPads and Prius's when both are dependent on a vast and destructive network.

As Hildebrand noted, Satanic pride is based upon a "blindness to value." This means that we value strip malls over farmland, that we build interstate interchanges that encourage sprawl rather than using city planning to sharpen the edges of city edges so that they do not encroach on farmland. It means that we value speed over community, convenience over art, "development" over preservation, McDonalds over meadowlarks. Such blindness may well be a part of our given, fallen nature, but it is developed through formative practices—the anti-spiritual disciplines of the fast and convenient.

6. Ibid.
7. Ibid., 11.

The greatest, and most damning discipline, is our use of money. It is through money that we have been able to abstract our understanding of value to the degree that we are willing to literally destroy our planet in order to get it. "Your money or your life" is too often answered, "my money." This reality has come to bear most notably in the discussions surrounding global climate change.

Oil and gas companies are working to tap all known reserves in order to get the profits out of the ground, but doing so will mean a rise in CO_2 well beyond the acceptable levels. Either the investors in these companies win or the globe does; we can't have it both ways. As Bill McKibben wrote in *Rolling Stone*:

> You can have a healthy fossil-fuel balance sheet, or a relatively healthy planet—but now that we know the numbers, it looks like you can't have both. Do the math: 2,795 (gigatons of carbon in the published worldwide reserves for oil, coal, and gas) is five times 565 (gigatons of carbon the atmosphere can absorb and maintain less than a 2 degrees Centigrade average global temperature increase). That's how the story ends.[8]

We have to make a decision as to whether we will continue to live as we do, but that decision will require us to abandon a great deal of money. Even if it might be worthless in the face of global climate calamity, the ideology of money is so powerful that many are simply unable to see outside of it. We are value-blind and so it is difficult for us to see our own demise, disciplined as we are in the money economy. We are like gamblers going broke for the win that will make it all worth it.

Being value-blind, we are also tempted to simply dismiss reality in order to accept our collective solipsism. This temptation is helped along by scientific ideologues such as Richard Dawkins, who wrote in an open letter to the Prince of Wales (in response to his opposition to genetic modification):

> The human brain, probably uniquely in the whole of evolutionary history, can see across the valley and can plot a course away from extinction and towards distant

8. McKibben, "New Math."

uplands. Long-term planning—and hence the very possibility of stewardship—is something utterly new on the
planet, even alien. It exists only in human brains. The
future is a new invention in evolution. It is precious. And
fragile. We must use all our scientific artifice to protect
it.[9]

For Dawkins Science (with a capital "S") will give us what we need
to both understand and reverse our long destruction, despite the
clear evidence that science has mostly been the handmaid to every
major destruction in the history of the world. This is not to say that
science, properly understood as specific knowledge, is bad, but we
have elevated science into a thing unto itself. It has been divorced
from limits and therefore from wisdom.

Science as a discipline is deeply tied into modernist ideologies.
Descartes, whose *Discourse on Method* served as the first significant
articulation of scientific reason, rushed the book to publication
because he was convinced that its methods of scientific reasoning
would lead to a significant extension of life, a cure Descartes hoped
would extend his own life. This goal is still a significant one—there
is still a great deal of scientific work that aims at prolonging life
indefinitely, with thinkers like Aubrey de Grey arguing for the possibility of indefinite life-extension through medical therapies.

Whether a cure for death is the goal or not, central to the
scientific ideology is power over nature. When Francis Bacon, Descartes' contemporary, wrote that "knowledge is power" (a slogan
adorning the walls of many a Middle School), he did not mean it in
some abstract sense. A man of the court, he meant that knowledge
is political power—a means of coercion.

Though science has certainly changed from the days of early ra-
tionalism, we have not strayed far from the central impulses that led
to modernism. This is largely clear in our education system where
science and math are, at least on the level of policy, emphasized
more heavily than literature or art. We are interested in science and
math, not because of our wonder and curiosity at the world, but because we hope that more scientists and mathematicians will secure

9. Dawkins, "Don't Turn Your Back."

increasing economic growth and American global supremacy, not to mention continuing military innovation.

It is interesting to note that the emphasis on the sciences has, deliberately or not, meant the demise of the humanities, disciplines which by their nature reach to the depths of human wisdom and understanding. Our interest is not wisdom, because wisdom does not mean power or a growing GDP. Reading *The Death of Ivan Ilyich* will not help promote economic growth—if anything it would do the opposite, calling people to see that a meaningful life cannot be found in wealth. If only Ivan Ilyich had known the wonders of modern medicine, perhaps he never would have had to face the deep questions of his meaning.

To confuse power with meaning, to confuse knowledge with wisdom, to not understand (to use Foucault's slash) that power/knowledge is the proper name for what we now mean by knowing, is the basic condition of industrial/technological society. No person perhaps exhibits this better than Freeman Dyson, a Nobel Prize-winning physicist. Dyson is a brilliant scientist, but he is also a deep doubter on the question of climate change. He is fundamentally against any effort to limit scientific and industrial progress in the name of protecting the "environment." Dyson has called environmentalism a "religion" rather than a science, but as Kenneth Brower writes in his profound profile of Dyson in *The Atlantic*, "The Danger of Cosmic Genius," Dyson misses his own faith commitments:

> "The main point [of environmentalism] is religious rather than scientific," he writes, yet never acknowledges that this proposition cuts both ways, never seems to recognize the extent to which his own arguments proceed from faith. Environmentalism worships the wisdom of Nature. Dysonism worships the indomitable ingenuity of Man. Dyson often suggests that science is on his side, but lately little of his popular exposition on planetary matters has anything to do with science . . . On the question of global warming, the world's climatologists and scientific institutions are almost unanimously arrayed against him. On his predictions for the future of ecosystems, ecologists beg to differ. Dysonian proclamations like "Now, after three billion years, the Darwinian interlude is over"

> are not science. (His argument here, which is that cultur-
> al evolution has replaced the Darwinian kind, is at best
> premature and at worst the craziest kind of hubris.)[10]

Dyson, a man who has exhibited brilliance across a number of scientific disciplines, is ending his career in a haze of blindness to reality—even scientific reality. Such is the danger of cosmic genius. After describing how a fellow scientist called Dyson's genius "cosmic," Brower writes at the close of his essay on Dyson, "The operative word for me is cosmic. The word terrestrial would not apply. In taking the measure of the universe, Dyson fails only in his appraisal of the small, spherical piece of the cosmos under his feet . . . For whatever reason, he is emotionally incapable of seeing the true colors of the rampant ingenuity of our species and calculating where our cleverness, as opposed to our wisdom, is taking us."[11]

This last line is particularly chilling, because it could be said for a great deal of our society, not only Dyson. Even environmentalists have, in a recent turn, centered their work on technological alternatives within the current system rather than a radical reorientation of society—gone is Edward Abbey and in his stead we have Adam Werbach, who would rather green Wal-Mart than wish its demise. We are powerfully wrapped up in a whole worldview in which human power and ingenuity are central.

We risk a great deal in this worldview. With such a claim to knowledge we will inevitably end up damaging our world, and eventually ourselves. As Wendell Berry wrote of the damage he inflicted on his hillside by trying to build a pond there, "The trouble was the familiar one: too much power, too little knowledge."[12] Berry had enough care, he had consulted the expert advice, what he lacked sufficiently was not care but fear.

Fear is an almost universally negative word in our culture. We are afraid of being afraid. But the only thing to fear is not fear itself. We should be afraid of never being afraid—fear is a powerful and necessary answer to our arrogant ignorance. If only we were

10. Brower, "Danger."

11. Ibid.

12. Berry, *What Are People*, 5.

more afraid of what might happen if we drill oil ever more deeply from the ocean floor. If only we were more afraid of the incredible power with which we play in every nuclear plant we build. If only we were more afraid of the coming climate catastrophe to admit that a slower economy is better than a global collapse.

The Hebrew wisdom tradition in particular praises proper fear: "the fear of the LORD is the beginning of wisdom" (Prov 9:10). This fear, as we have said, is not terror—it is a proper respect for real and dangerous power. To fear the LORD means to not play fast and loose with God; to spend a good deal of time worrying that we are right with God. Fear of the Lord is, in other words, the opposite of hubris—it is humility.

St. Benedict places a sense of this fear as the beginning of his "ladder of humility" as articulated in his rule for monks. "The first step of humility, then, is that we keep 'the reverence of God always before our eyes' (Ps. 36:2) and never forget it."[13] It is only when we move away from this reverence that we begin to fall into the hubris that leads to destruction. This is not to say that we will always be perfect in our reverence, but what matters is the trajectory of our lives—that we never forget it. As St. Benedict writes at the end of the explanation of this first rung of the ladder, "God is loving and waits for us to improve."[14]

This point is important as we begin to seek a way of living that moves beyond hubris. We are ignorant, and we are doomed to fail, even when we know that what we are doing is wrong. We are often caught up in sinful systems that do not allow us to seek the good in a full way. For instance, though we believe that plastics are deeply destructive and that the world would be a better place without them, it is difficult, if not impossible, to live life in the modern world without them. We can reduce our use, but we cannot be completely free of them without so radically leaving society that we would be of little use.

Wendell Berry speaks of this problem in regard to his use of a car. There are few people who are more uncomfortable with the oil

---

13. In Chittister, *Rule*, 63.
14. Ibid., 65.

economy than Berry. Yet he drives a vehicle because, as he has said, he doesn't know how to be neighborly without one.

The key difference between Berry and the person who commutes an hour and half in a SUV is that Berry is not comfortable with his choice. It is a choice that troubles him and one that he hopes will continue to trouble him. This is what reverence gives us—we move and live, time-bound and ignorant, in the world, but we always do so with fear and trembling.

In order to achieve individual goodness we must work for the good of the commonwealth. If we are in a society that prevents us from being good, we must change that society so that we have the choice for goodness. For instance, if we believe that the only way to achieve care for animals and the land is to have animals raised on small farms, then we must also ensure that the state's legal structure makes such farming possible, particularly in regards to slaughtering and butchering the animals. There are many places where state regulations make it very difficult to produce good meat in a cost effective way. The same might go for raw dairy. Customers should have the ability to buy what food they deem healthy directly from farmers without the intervention of the state.

In these kinds of arguments many people think that agrarians are simply libertarians—removing the barriers so that individuals can make the right choices. But this is far from the case. No agrarian would allow anyone to do whatever they please with land, air, or water, to name a few parts of the commonwealth. Agrarians would hold such spaces to a high standard of use and would surely restrict access to those who might harm these common goods.

This is all to say that if we are to live in reverence we must be able to make structural changes in order to do so. But again, these structural changes are not made without their own fear, their own sense that we are acting in ignorance. We must always worry that we do not know the way.

St. Benedict's second step of humility offers an opportunity to move beyond this stasis. This step is that "we love not our own will nor take pleasure in the satisfaction of our desires; rather we shall imitate by our actions that saying of Christ's: 'I have come not to do my own will, but the will of the One who sent me' (John 6:38)."[15] This brings us to what is essentially a question of freedom—there are two wills available, of which we can take only one.

Paul articulated this idea in Romans 6:16: "Do you not know that if you present yourselves to anyone as obedient slaves, you are slaves of the one whom you obey, either of sin, which leads to death, or of obedience, which leads to righteousness?" For agrarians we might rewrite the verse to say, "Do you not know that you are a slave to the ones upon which you depend, Exxon and Shell, Apple and Monstanto, which lead to violence and death, or to the creation which leads to beauty and health?" This may seem like too much, but it is not far from the truth. When agrarians talk about nature, they speak of nature as their master and teacher—Gene Logsdon describes the goal of his farming as being work at "nature's pace." It is hubris to believe that we are not mastered by systems, that we are not controlled by ideologies. Our task is to be mastered by what is good, to enslave ourselves to what will be our salvation.

In doing this we return to the idea that we are creatures, which skipping ahead a bit brings us to the sixth step in Benedict's ladder of humility: "The sixth step of humility is that we are content with the lowest and most menial treatment, and regard ourselves as a poor and worthless worker in whatever task we are given, saying with the prophet: 'I am insignificant and ignorant, not better than a beast before you, yet I am with you always' (Ps. 73:22–23)."[16]

Much has been made of the Hebrew and Christian scripture's emphasis on what's been called "dominion" as the roots of our environmental crisis, and while there is some responsibility to bear from some Christian groups, passages like the above do not lead to the idea of complete mastery over the earth. If we all sought this kind of humility that says "I am insignificant and ignorant, no better than a beast" it is unlikely that we would have arrived at the kind of crisis we now face. Instead, this crisis is the result of a modernist cult of technological progress, driven in large part by the desire to increase profits for a few. Christians, at their best, have always stood

15. Ibid., 66.
16. Ibid., 69.

in the way of such progress whether it was calling for better conditions for workers, more equitable property relationships, or care for God's creatures. It is only when Christians have been unfaithful, baptizing the beliefs of economic progressives, that they have lent their moral authority to those bent on destruction.

Rather than fleeing from biblical views of creation we should embrace them more fully, not simply living in the light of Genesis, but the full biblical witness that shows, again and again, a creation that God loves and a people who are ignorant and lost without God's limits, discipline, and guidance.

An Economics of Humility

So, living in a fear of the Lord, realizing the limits of our power and the power of our ignorance, what would a humble economy look like? How would we structure an economy that lives beyond hubris, that lives in the truth and is not blind to value? It would be moving against our efforts at a humble economy to say that such an economy could be outlined in full, but we might be able to offer a few features that would be included in such an economy.

The first of these would be that this would be an economy made of glass—an economy of complete transparency. It is interesting to note here that open faces are often the marks of saints—their faces, like children's, do not hide what is inside. It would be the same in an economy of humility—the inside would be as visible as the outside. There would be no wondering where my computer came from, how the metals were mined, who was involved and who profited—every aspect would be easily available to clear sight.

Agrarian journalist Michael Pollan, in *The Omnivore's Dilemma*, suggests that the meat industry follow such transparency:

> Sometimes I think that all it would take to clarify our feelings about eating meat, and in the process begin to redeem animal agriculture, would be to simply pass a law requiring all the sheet-metal walls of all the CAFOs, and even the concrete walls of slaughterhouses, to be

replaced by glass. If there's any new right we need to establish, maybe this is the one: the right, I mean, to look.[17]

If we cannot bear to look at every aspect of our economic life then we should not participate in it. But in order to look, we must be able to see. For so much of our economic life we simply can't see. This is not simply because of our own blindness; it is also because the reality of what we buy and sell, the reality of what we earn, is hidden from us.

There are even whole series of laws and statutes that keep us from seeing what the reality around us really is. Most farms are protected, by law, from citizens seeing what they do and how they do it. In states like Pennsylvania, Monsanto has been successful in lobbying for legislation that would keep consumers from knowing whether hormones were used in the production of their milk. In Pennsylvania and Ohio, doctors are restricted from telling patients about the health risks of living near hydraulic fracturing gas mining operations.

The industrial economy, like any power or person who lies, relies on secrecy, invisibility, and dissimulation. An agrarian economy, an economy of humility, must answer this with visibility and openness. The agrarian economy is one that invites participation by all the parties involved—the farmer and the customer, the butcher and the grocer, all are invited to see the entirety of the process. This will inevitably mean that not all will look pretty.

We must realize that a great deal of work has gone into creating illusions surrounding the sources of our food. One goes to the grocery store and the brand names almost always have an agrarian tie—farm, ranch, etc. The colorful packaging are all there to tell us a story that invokes deep childhood imaginings about farm life—devoid of all reality. We all but see a jolly old farmer with a talking pig. If we stopped to consider all of this for a moment, we would be insulted, but it all seems normal. Marketers treat us like children and we are happy to accept the role.

The "adult" reality isn't much better though. Agriculture companies do all they can to hide what they are doing through divisions

17. Pollan, *Omnivore's Dilemma*, 332.

of labor—the marketing manager never goes to the kill floor, the chicken farmer has no say in packaging. On the one hand we have the happy image of a chicken who lived its life on "happy acres" with a friend named Bessy the Cow and one day was magically transfigured into packages of low-fat white meat without the messiness of death. On the other hand, we have corporate statements about the sales of their "protein solutions."

There is a farm whose meat I eat frequently that advertises the days it is going to kill chickens. Come, kill your chicken, and bring one home! That is the message of an agrarian economy. Here we must face the reality of the food we eat—see the chicken's eyes looking back before we slit its throat with the decisive cut, feel the warmth of its blood against our hand, reach inside and draw out it entrails. I have done this hundreds of times, and yet when I look at a plastic-wrapped chicken breast in a grocery store it is hard to see the reality—I cannot imagine the chicken's look and that look is essential for humility, because it is what calls us to our measure. Who are you to kill and eat? That is the question of any animal's eyes before its death.

Wonder is another essential feature of the humble economy—wonder is a way of experiencing and knowing that one does not propose to comprehend the totality of a thing. The opposite of wonder is boredom, which comes when we are no longer amazed by the facts. In wonder the world is vast, mysterious, questioning, and our existence within it is small, limited, yet magical. In wonder we don't know everything there is to know and yet we hunger to know and understand. Desire is an essential feature of wonder and yet it is a desire that we don't propose to complete.

Wonder is second-grade science not tenth-grade science—children are full of wonder because they propose to know so little and what they want to know is of so little use. In many elementary schools, science at the youngest grades centers on building curiosity. It is often children's favorite subject. While the best teachers are able to carry this through the higher grades, too often science becomes the boring repetition of facts divorced from wonder and meaning alike. When I taught high school students, I would often ask them about what they were learning in science. They would mostly produce flash cards with terms that the students could recite but not understand. True "natural science," an exploration of the world of natural phenomena, should be a be a subject of wonder, but it has been turned by state standards and the demands of an educated work force into as boring a reality as a corporate financial statement. The same goes for math. Both math and science, so prized in technological society, have been reduced from disciplines of wonder to disciplines of utility—the best work in both fields are still done by those for whom their work has no promise of profit. Galileo, Newton, Kepler, and Copernicus—these are the true scientists, filled with the wonder of their subjects and pursuing knowledge useless to the general public. It is notable too that many of these scientist mixed what we would call magic and mystery with their pursuit of the raw facts of nature. Kepler was clearly as interested in astrology as astronomy and Newton was bent on unraveling the mysteries of the Book of Revelation, a task as important in his mind as the calculus.

Several years ago I heard a scientist named Joe Lewis on NPR who exhibited the true discipline of wonder. His research had a very practical outcome—he had trained wasps to identify bombs. But when asked about the broader lessons about insects and smell he said, "There once was a staying 'The deeper the well, the sweeter the honey.' Indeed, there was a time—and let me say, early in my profession that if I had talked about insects having this capability, I would have been laughed out of my profession . . . But as we move along and find what we're seeing, that learning in this highly sophisticated ability to integrate taste and smell and to quickly link and utilize these type of things is a much more primitive ability than we had imagined. In their world and on their territory, they are as sophisticated as we are. And they've been around a long, long time."

To this the reporter responded, "I'll never look at [wasps] the same way."

"Each day, I find that I look at them with much greater respect. In many ways, all these things are rather sacred," said Lewis in reply.[18]

18. Block, "Wasps."

All these things are rather sacred. This is the response of wonder—not a response of totalizing knowledge but of deeper mystery, what we know only opens up the vastness of what we don't. Humility places us here so we can marvel. True discovery opens up awe, while exploration is directed at the end of conquest.

A Tentative Prejudice

Humility, recognizing our place and dependence upon the earth, also brings into question the prejudices of our history and culture. The person who sees herself as she really is will unlikely put much stock in her first judgments. Prejudice, of course, is a necessary feature of human engagement with the world. If we didn't have a prejudice against snakes, we might die. Even though not all snakes are bad and we should certainly celebrate their existence, it is good to pause before picking one up. But prejudices that are unchallenged and unchangeable are dangerous. Prejudice is not to be justice, our final understanding; it is simply an entry point in the world. Humility helps discipline prejudice so that we do not take the easy path, and simply accept our prejudices as justice, rather than doing the difficult work of understanding.

Humility means both that we don't presume to go against the traditions that have come before but also that we don't presume that those traditions are always right. Agrarianism, in the same way, is not against innovations in agriculture. With nature as its constant measure and pattern, agrarian life must always be experimental. Most good farmers I know are constantly testing and experimenting, trying to find the right way to farm in the unique conditions of their place. Those who are farming using the radical, techoscientific methods of geneticists and chemists are in a way the most conservative. There is a magazine called *Progressive Farmer* that promotes modern industrial agriculture, but its pages are filled with the most staid advice—standardized and formulaic rather than experimental and specific to varied places.

Diversified farms, which is to say, historically grounded farms, are able to experiment. The large "scientific" monocultural farms however are risk averse to the extreme. Their systems are so fixed that farmers are hesitant to try anything new and because these farms are so saddled with debt such a risk would be impossible. These farms are left living on razor-thin margins, and all experimentation and innovation is left with the companies who are willing to sell them "solutions." These farmers are, as one reformed rancher told me, using credit instead of their brains.

The status quo is a powerful force, especially when the weight of our self understanding is tied up with it. Yet an openness occurs when we see our significance framed in a larger world. This is what happened to Job when God appeared to him in the whirlwind. God unsettled Job's prejudice toward his own place in the world—God humiliated him, brought him to a place close to the earth, and allowed Job to see his smallness in a vast and wonder-filled creation. We are told at the end of the book that Job divided his inheritance among all of his children, both sons and daughters—an unheard of action in the ancient Near East.

When we accept that we come from dirt, are dependent upon dirt, will return to dirt, then our orientation toward the world becomes different. At the same time we find the freedom to experiment and open ourselves to the new, but we also lose our pretensions to having it all figured out. This also leads us into a kind of slowness; a different relationship with time. This different relationship with time keeps us from thinking that we must accomplish everything now, that the burdens of the world must be solved tomorrow. Patience is a virtue that is the close complement of humility.

Patience and humility are no better paired than in the God-Human Christ. In Christ we see a God who is willing to suffer death through love rather than exercise the expedience of violence. The so-called problem of evil is not a problem of evil so much as it is a problem of speed. The way the problem goes is how can a good and omnipotent God allow for evil to exist in the world, but the answer is the same as it is for his children. How can good people allow evil dictators to go on killing and brutalizing their people? And the answer is that we are unwilling to exercise violence in order to achieve our goals. This does not mean that we turn our backs on the suffering—instead the Christian response is to go and suffer with them, opposing with our very life the evil that is perpetrated against them. This is the way of Christ who came and suffered the rejection of love, even to the brutal death on a cross, in solidarity with all those good people who suffer from evil, death, and decay. Resurrection, not redemptive violence, is the Christian way, and to resurrect we must first be put to death.

We must always keep our commitment to reality, as exposed through love, even if that commitment means that we must be willing to let people die for our unwillingness to violate it. There may be people who die because we are unwilling to use certain technologies or violate certain limits. We must be willing for that to happen because we are committed to a higher love. But in this we do not turn our backs—we follow Christ to the cross of solidarity, we suffer with them and him, in patient longing for the complete redemption of the world. This is the radical position of the humble who will inherit the earth.

To give an example of what we mean here let me recount a recent discussion I had with some friends. One friend was talking about the coming global crisis of refrigeration—refrigerators are constant energy drains and tend to redefine traditional lifestyles in techno-capitalistic ways. It is simply unsustainable for everyone in the world to have refrigerators—they are one of the most toxic parts of our daily life. But there is a global push for more refrigerators in countries with large populations like India and such large-scale expansion will result in a massive raising of greenhouse gas emissions. Another friend, however, brought up a project that she was working with to help bring refrigerated transport to Bangladesh. With refrigerated transport a great deal more food would be distributed to poor Bangladeshis who would otherwise be seriously malnourished if not starving.

So how do we move out of such an impasse? I have no easy answers but I can say that through continuing the expansion of refrigerators we are only violating, more and more deeply, the reality of our world—the inviolable limits of creation. This does not mean that we must not work to alleviate the suffering of those who are starving—we should in fact do all we can to work, and suffer alongside them, but we must not do it at the expense of violating a deeper love. The industrial economy sells itself on the necessary compromises of answering the needs we have now. The economy of humility, in the practice of radical patience, says we will wait. We will trust in God's goodness and the path of obedience.

This faithful patience also helps to free us from what is one of the most powerful animators of the industrial economy—envy. Humility turns our attention to ourselves, our work, our life in light of the life upon which we are modeled—Christ. The Amish offer an excellent example of the practice of this humility. As philosopher Slavoj Zizek articulates it:

> The difference between the authentic fundamentalists and the perverted Moral Majority fundamentalists is that the first (like the Amish in the United States) get along very well with their American neighbors since they are simply centered on their own world and not bothered by what goes on out there among "them," while the Moral Majority fundamentalist is always haunted by the ambiguous attitude of horror/envy with regard to the unspeakable pleasures in which the sinners engage. The reference to Envy as one of the seven deadly sins can thus serve as a perfect instrument enabling us to distinguish authentic fundamentalism from its Moral Majority mockery: authentic fundamentalists do not envy their neighbors, their different *jouissance*.[19]

This does not mean that the authentic fundamentalists are disengaged from the world as many mistakenly think the Amish are. The Amish have served, in similar ways to monastic communities in the medieval period, to preserve sane ways of life amidst the insanity of the outside world. Many people are now going to the Amish to learn simple and sane living. They have been providing just that in the form of sharing everything from traditional farming knowledge to providing all but forgotten horse-drawn tools to sustainable farmers who want to return to animal power rather than using fossil fuel guzzling tractors. Some Amish, such as David Kline, are even active in more outward ways such as the publication of *Farming* magazine,

19. Zizek, *Belief*, 68.

which is filled with traditional farming knowledge and key agrarian essays by writers such as Gene Logsdon and Wendell Berry.

The Amish critique of the larger society often comes in the form of a quiet contrast—their slowness in their buggys going down the highway amidst speeding traffic. I once read a story that illustrates this point well. In many parts of Ohio and Pennsylvania Amish communities are being overtaken by suburban sprawl. In one such community, a family was moving into a large suburban home next to an Amish farmer. The Amishman, committed to being a good neighbor, helped the family unload their moving van. They brought in dishwashers, refrigerators, televisions, computers, and a host of other electric appliances that the Amishman, without the convenience of electricity, would have no use for. It was a surprise then, when the Amishman, at the end of the day before returning to his farm said, "If any of this stuff breaks, let me know." Taken aback, the newcomer said, "You mean you know how to fix these kinds of things?" "I wouldn't know the first thing about fixing any of that stuff," the Amishman said with a smile, "but I can show you how to live without it all." That is the authentic and humble response—a life that is lived authentically, close to reality, and ready to be useful to those who would wish to join that path.

Conclusion

Humility is being brought low, close to the earth—the soil from which we were formed and to which we will return. To live authentic lives, lives that are both truthful and real, we must be disciplined by the realities of that soil. We must remember that however powerful we might become, it is upon the dirt that we are dependent and our goodness might be measured by whether our actions build or destroy this fundamental reality. It is tempting to believe that we know enough, that we are not plagued by ignorance. This temptation is aided by the insulated lives we create, solipsisms that ignore the framework that makes life possible. Even for cyberspace, for the most virtual of our realities, the entire system would crash without the grounded realities of mines, of food, of dirt. Without these, all of our technology and power is but a flicker on the screen.

In order to recover humility against the temptations of hubris we must learn to fear again—to be cautious, to worry that our way might not be good enough. It is not only on the scale of individuals that our society has become hooked on Zoloft and Prozac, we are collectively popping the pills that will keep us from the anxiety that will save us. Let's start to worry, let us walk with fear and trembling, and then find peace in the reality that we have been ignoring—we are not God.

Epilogue

Cultivation of the Heart

We began our explorations of the agrarian habit of mind with the hope that if we *thought* closer to the soil, we might be saved. In exploring how agrarianism approaches time and humility, property and the body we have hopefully been moved toward freedom from the industrial mind and found ourselves more deeply rooted in the soil in which we will flourish. But to adopt this better way of seeing and thinking is not enough. We need the long slow work of cultivating our hearts.

We won't be able to gain freedom from the destruction of industrialism if our hearts are not fundamentally reworked so that our desires fit more and more closely with what we've seen to be good and true. For this work to happen we need a community that learns to tell the truth and practice it. In order to live into reality we need the church.

My own life is far from the beautiful and disciplined existence I often hope for. It is a messy life, same as any, filled with contradictions and compromises I would hate to admit. I do not always eat as I wish I did. I do not hunt and fish and grow all of my food or even buy it all from local farmers. My life is lost in plastic wrap and gasoline. I have tried hard to live otherwise, but the pressures are greater than my ability alone.

It is only in the church that I or any of us have any real hope of having our hearts cultivated toward reality. A church, for all of its failings, for all of the distortions of many communities, might seem a poor place to achieve what agrarianism cannot complete, but I'm afraid there is no other choice.

We need to keep coming together, keep trying to open ourselves to the change Jesus offered if we would only follow his way of death and life. There is always another season if this one failed; always one more chance to begin to plant and grow in abundance. We have forever, so why not get to work now?

Acknowledgements

A book like this one is made through many conversations and so I want to start by acknowledging a few of my conversation partners. Fred Bahnson graciously read and commented on drafts of these chapters as well as carrying on a handwritten correspondence that has been deeply enriching. Chris Smith and Englewood Christian Church have continued to enliven my imagination and my reading. The Ekklesia Project has given me many friends and one weekend of deep conversations that often give me enough to think about until the next summer's gathering. Thanks to Rodney Clapp, Heather Carraher, Caitlin Mackenzie and all those at Wipf and Stock who helped bring this book to completion. Most of all I want to thank my wife Emily, who has read every word, called me to be better, and continually reminds me that God is love.

Bibliography

Bailey, Liberty Hyde. *The Holy Earth*. Reprinted with foreword by Ragan Sutterfield. Indianapolis: Doulos Christou, 2008. First published 1916 by Scribners.

Benson, Bruce. "Jean-Luc Marion Tests the Limits of Logic." *The Christian Century* (February 8, 2003) 22–25.

Bernard, of Clairvaux. *The Steps of Humility and Pride*. Kalamazoo, MI: Cistercian Publications, 1989.

Berger, John. *Selected Essays: John Berger*. Edited by Geoff Dyer. New York: Vintage, 2001.

Berry, Wendell. *Another Turn of the Crank: Essays*. Berkeley: Counterpoint, 2001.

———. *Citizenship Papers*. Washington, DC: Shoemaker & Hoard, 2003.

———. *The Gift of Good Land: Further Essays Cultural and Agricultural*. New York: North Point, 1982.

———. *Home Economics: Fourteen Essays*. New York: North Point, 1987.

———. *That Distant Land: The Collected Stories*. Washington, DC: Shoemaker & Hoard, 2004.

———. *The Unsettling of America: Culture & Agriculture*. San Francisco: Sierra, 1977.

———. *The Way of Ignorance*. Washington, DC: Shoemaker & Hoard, 2005.

———. *What Are People For?: Essays*. New York: North Point, 1990.

Block, Melissa. "Wasps Used to Detect Explosives." *All Things Considered, NPR*, December 5, 2005.

Bonhoeffer, Dietrich. *No Rusty Swords*. New York: Harper & Row, 1965.

Braungart, Michael. "Quote of the Day: Michael Braungart on Population." *TreeHugger.com* (August 29, 2008). No pages. Online: http://www.treehugger.com/sustainable-product-design/quote-of-the-day-michael-braungart-on-population.html.

Brower, Kenneth. "The Danger of Cosmic Genius." *The Atlantic*, December 2010. Online: http://www.theatlantic.com/magazine/archive/2010/12/the-danger-of-cosmic-genius/308306/.

Capon, Robert Farrar. *The Supper of the Lamb: A Culinary Reflection*. New York: Harcourt, 1969.

Bibliography

Cayley, David. *The Rivers North of the Future: The Testament of Ivan Illich.* Toronto : House of Anansi, 2004.

Chittister, Joan. *The Rule of Benedict: Insights for the Ages.* New York: Crossroad, 1992.

Dawkins, Richard. "Don't Turn Your Back on Science: An Open Letter to Prince Charles." *The Observer,* May 20, 2000. Online: http://www.guardian.co.uk/science/2000/may/21/gm.food1.

Hauerwas, Stanley and John Berkman. "The Chief End of All Flesh." *Theology Today* 49:2 (July 1992) 196–206.

Heschel, Abraham Joshua. *The Sabbath: Its Meaning for Modern Man.* New York: Farrar, Straus, and Giroux, 1951.

Jacobs, Jane. *Dark Age Ahead.* New York: Vintage, 2004.

Johnson, Kelly S. *The Fear of Beggars: Stewardship and Poverty in Christian Ethics.* Grand Rapids: Eerdmans, 2007.

Kerouac, Jack. *On the Road.* New York: Penguin, 1957

Kidd, Chip. "Designing Books is No Laughing Matter. OK, It Is." Filmed March 2012. TED video, 17:16. Posted April 2012. Online: http://www.ted.com/talks/chip_kidd_designing_books_is_no_laughing_matter_ok_it_is.html.

King, F. H. *Farmers of Forty Centuries or Permanent Agriculture in China, Korea and Japan.* 1911. Reprint, Mineola, NY: Dover, 2004.

Koyama, Kosuke. *Water Buffalo Theology.* Maryknoll, NY: Orbis, 1999.

Kundera, Milan. *The Unbearable Lightness of Being.* Translated by Michael Henry Heim. New York: Harper, 1984.

Lawler, Peter Augustine. "Luther, Locke, Liberty, and the American Founding Fathers." *Mars Hill Audio Journal* v. 71, November/December 2004

Locke, John. *Two Treatises on Government.* London: Butler etc., 1821. (Digitized by Google).

Logsdon, Gene. *The Gardener's Guide to Better Soil.* Emmaus, PA: Rodale, 1975.

————. *Holy Shit: Managing Manure to Save Mankind.* White River Junction, VT: Chelsea Green, 2010.

————. *Living at Nature's Pace: Farming and the American Dream.* White River Junction, VT: Chelsea Green, 2000.

MacIntyre, Alasdair. *After Virtue.* 3rd ed. South Bend, IN: University of Notre Dame Press, 2007.

McKibben, Bill. "Global Warming's Terrifying New Math." *Rolling Stone,* July 19, 2012. Online: http://www.rollingstone.com/politics/news/global-warmings-terrifying-new-math-20120719.

Nabhan, Gary. *The Desert Smells Like Rain: A Naturalist in O'odham Country.* Tucson: University of Arizona Press, 2002.

Neighmond, Patti. "To Sniff Out Childhood Allergies, Researchers Head to the Farm." *Shots* (Blog), *NPR,* June 11, 2012, http://www.npr.org/blogs/health/2012/06/12/154593662/to-sniff-out-childhood-allergies-researchers-head-to-the-farm.

Pollan, Michael. *The Omnivore's Dilemma: A Natural History of Four Meals.* New York: Penguin, 2006.

Radio Free Babylon. "World Peace." Online Comic: http://radiofreebabylon. com/RFB%20Images/CoffeeWithJesus/coffeewithjesus249.jpg

Robinson, Marilynne. *The Death of Adam: Essays on Modern Thought.* New York: Mariner, 2000.

Roz, Guy and Brent Baugman. "Ranchers' Land Becomes Ground Zero in Energy Fight." *NPR* (Online), February 25, 2012, http://www.npr. org/2012/02/25/147413520/ranchers-land-becomes-ground-zero-in-energy-fight.

"Steve Paxton," YouTube Video, 4:21, posted by "droppingapproved," December 21, 2009, http://youtu.be/a82Qy62bUTc.

Voison, Andre. *Fertilizer Application: Soil, Plant, Animal.* London: Crosby Lockwood, 1965.

Von Hildebrand. *Humility: Wellspring of Virtue.* Manchester, NH: Sophia Institute, 1990.

Watson, Lyall. *The Whole Hog: Exploring the Extraordinary Potential of Pigs.* Washington: Smithsonian, 2004

Willard, Dallas. *Renovation of the Heart: Putting on the Character of Christ.* Colorado Springs: NavPress, 2002.

Zizek, Slavoj. *The Fragile Absolute, or, Why Is the Christian Legacy Worth Fighting For?* New York: Verso, 2000.

———. *On Belief.* New York: Routledge, 2001.

27308920R00077